What I Need to Know About Marketing

Also by David A. Stone

Books (in print)

[re]wired: Selling Your AE Services in a Post-Recession World
Nothing Happens Till Somebody Sells Something (Volume 1)
Nothing Happens Till Somebody Sells Something (Volume 2)
Nothing Happens Till Somebody Sells Something (Volume 3)

Audio Recording
The Negotiation Waltz

Video Recordings
How bad do you want it?
Going for gold
Nailed it!
Writing in teams
Find your business development strength
Profitable marketing
Own their eyeballs
The half-time marketing checkup
Making it rain
The crystal ball session
Five steps to proposal success
Keeping clients for life
The master class in business networking
Build your slam-dunk marketing plan
The entrepreneurial project manager
How marketing works
Sealing the deal
Launch! Your marketing year

What I Need to Know About Marketing

DAVID A. STONE

Brisa Books
An imprint of
The WindWord Group Publishing & Media, LLC
Savannah GA

The WindWord Group Publishing & Media
Suite 200, 100 Bull Street
Savannah, GA 31401 USA
www.windwordgroup.com
Brisa Books, an imprint of The WindWord Group
ISBN-10: 0-9983990-7-8
ISBN-13: 978-0-9983990-7-2

Please contact the publisher regarding large-quantity book purchases, interviews, or speaking requests
www.windwordgroup.com email admin@windwordgroup.com

Printed in the United States of America

Some portions of the contents of this book may have appeared previously in online content on David Stone's website and in other collections of his columns and blogs.

DAVID A. STONE

For Gail, who keeps me moving relentlessly forward, but who taught me that it's also ok to pause, rest or even stop altogether.

Introduction

Forty-three years is a long time. And when you look up and see that you've spent the better part of half a century participating in and observing something, you realize that you've formed some opinions. Opinions and observations that, invited or not, you'd like to share.

The design and construction industry have undergone enormous changes since I began my career. Some have been enormously positive – the advent of computer-aided design and modeling have allowed architects and engineers like Frank Gehry and Santiago Calatrava to create buildings and structures that were simply impossible on a drafting board. Modern materials and technologies allow buildings, structures and processes to operate more efficiently and effectively than ever before.

On the down side, liability exposure has exploded for the designer and contractor, resulting in lawyer-induced procedures that add tremendous cost.

Perhaps the biggest change, though, has been the explosive increase in competition. Where, in 1975, there may have been half a dozen firms competing for any given project, today it's not uncommon to have ten times that many submit viable, competitive proposals.

The last 30 years of my career have been spent helping firms deal with this intense competition. As an industry, we've had to learn to market, to create and leverage competitive advantage and to communicate the benefits a client receives rather than the features a firm offers. In a profession that prides itself on empiricism and facts, this has frequently felt a little too touchy-feely for comfort. It's far easier to talk about the merits of your work than warm fuzzy notions about client perception. But that doesn't work anymore.

This book is a collection of the observations and thoughts I've had over the last three decades and the advice that I've passed along to AE firms of every size, shape and configuration imaginable. It's sometimes counterintuitive to the left-brained among us, but this stuff works.

If you want to sell your design services, this is what you need to know.

Table of Contents

Marketing resolutions

Wanna grow?

If not, why are you in business?

If so, here are the three most powerful marketing resolutions you can make to guarantee new clients, new projects and solid growth.

1. Develop a written marketing plan

There's an old saying that veteran project managers will tell the newbies: "If it isn't written down, it didn't happen." That adage applies to looking backwards. Looking ahead has a similar truth: "If it isn't written down, it ain't going to happen." If you have a written marketing plan, you WILL execute at least part of it and you WILL get results.

Your plan doesn't have to be lengthy and detailed. In fact, the shorter, the more specific and the more action-oriented the better. "We are going to grow in this specific market, targeting these specific client groups. We are going to use these specific actions, every week, in the pursuit of that growth. We are going to use these specific metrics to track our progress." If it takes more than two pages, it's too long.

2. Turn down one of every three opportunities that cross your desk

Seriously. You're not going to grow if you keep taking shots at everything that moves. Focus on your target, aim carefully and drive your hit rate up.

Instead of writing 10 proposals and winning two or three, write only five and win the same two or three. But wait! If you only write five, suddenly you have more time, more resources, more focus t make that particular proposal sound like it was written to that particular client instead of bland boilerplate that was flung at the wall in hopes it would stick.

While counterintuitive, the simple act of responding to fewer RFPs will raise your hit rate, reduce your marketing costs and dramatically improve the quality of your submittals.

3.   Have at least two meals a week with someone outside your firm
Most of us eat 21 meals each week. I know one particularly gifted business developer who sets a goal of sharing 15 of them with clients and other business contacts. Guess what kind of success he has in bringing in work.

Let's say that your small business has 12 people who include 'business development' in their list of responsibilities. If each of those 12 people took two people to lunch (or breakfast or dinner) each week, that's 24 meals per week or 1,248 over the course of the year. Run your own numbers for your business. Now look me in the eye and tell me that 1200 meals won't turn into new opportunities, new relationships, new contacts and new work!

If the cost of each lunch is $35, that's $43,680 in the year. Who's got that kind of money? The firm that stopped spending it on wasted proposals in which they didn't have any relationship with the client. The average cost of assembling a competitive proposal is about $7,500. Pass on six proposals and you've paid for all the lunches.

Marketing is not difficult.   A few simple actions, repeated regularly will produce dramatic results. Stop thinking about it. Stop planning to plan. Stop circling around it. Start doing it.

Keep your cash flowing

O h, how times have changed! In the architecture, engineering, environmental consulting, and construction industries that I've studied, where many clients used to pay within a few weeks, many now typically wait 45, 90 and even 120 days or more to pay their bills. That's a problem because cash flow affects everything your firm does. Here are some tips for dealing with it.

Terms of payment must always be in your contract including invoice frequency and the time of the month when your bill will be sent. If, for example, they process bills on the 20th of every month, find out when the invoice must be in to be included in the cycle.

Also settle the format of your invoice during negotiations including the precise information they want included. Attach a sample copy of an invoice, initialed by the client, as an exhibit in the contract.

Get your invoices out on time. If you've negotiated to invoice by the 10th of every month, get the bills out by the 10th! Why should the client honor a payment schedule if you can't stick to the billing schedule?

Call them five days after the invoice is sent to confirm they've received it. The number one excuse for delayed payment: "I never received it, please send it again."

During that call, ask if they have any questions or concerns. The number two excuse for delayed payment: "I'm glad you called (now that the invoice is overdue!). I have some problems with this bill that we need to discuss." Call after five days and remove the top two reasons for delayed payments.

Rattle their cage with a polite 'reminder' call when the bill is just 10 days overdue. Waiting a month will delay any action for another 30 days.

When the invoice is 20 days overdue call and ask if there is any problem. Tell them how much you want this project to succeed and ask when you can expect to receive a check.

When it's 30 days overdue request a personal meeting to discuss the problem or offer to send a courier to pick up the check.

At 45 days write a letter stating your "serious concern." Review the steps you've taken to collect and any payment promises they've made. Issue a velvet-covered threat by offering to "pause the work if cash flow is a temporary problem" for them.

When it's 60 days overdue slow the pace of the work considerably but don't stop. Don't respond to inquiries and issue no progress documents. Send a sternly worded letter stating that all work is about to cease and the issue will be handed over to legal counsel for collections.

When the invoice is 75 days overdue stop all work and have your lawyer send a letter of intention to lien. At 90 days, file a lien.

Never offer a discount or change the payment terms as an inducement to pay. That only teaches your client that, if they wait long enough, you'll lower the price.

Hard nosed? You bet! Many firms tell me, "We don't want to offend them," or, "They might get mad and not hire us again." These are excuses to avoid confrontation. If they're offended at being asked to stick to the terms of a contract they signed, this isn't a client you want. And if you're afraid they might not hire you again, consider this: You wanted them to hire you so they'd pay you. They're not paying you. Why would you want them to hire you again?

Taking out the head trash

Henry Ford, one of the great innovators of the last century, once famously said, "Whether you think you can or you can't, you're right." In other words, the only obstacle to your success is your firm belief that the odds that are stacked against you are insurmountable.

Despite the delightful fact that the recession is quickly fading in the rear view mirror, the world we've inherited is vastly different than the one we left behind. The rules have changed dramatically and it's making a lot of professionals uncomfortable.

I've been hearing it every day:

"Clients don't have the same loyalty they used to!"

"The competition is red hot!"

"The big firms have come to town and they're eating up all the projects!"

"We've lost at least four great projects that should have been ours!"

It's both easy and convenient to place blame. The clients who fail to understand your value, the competitors who undercut your fees, even the planets that fail to align in your favor. Regardless of whose fault you declare it to be, when the dust has settled, the challenges remain leaving you with two choices. Give up and go home. Or find some way to climb over, knock down or bust through the wall that blocks your path.

The wall you're facing right now is called 'change.' It's the need for you to accept that the strategies and tactics that got your firm this far aren't going to get you much farther in this strange new world.

I've seen so much resistance to change that I could sell it by the pound. Excuses fly thick and fast and the rationalizing that explains why the status quo is the best plan could float a ship. I find it particularly disturbing that most (but by no means all) of the resistance is coming from my fellow baby boomers who spent their youth fighting the establishment and preaching revolution.

If we accept that 'ol Henry was right, then the change that must be made begins by taking out the trash that's in your head. Every time you catch yourself thinking that something is unlikely, improbable or impossible, stop. Catch yourself, think about Nelson Mandela, Martin Luther King and Helen Keller, and then ask yourself if your little challenge is truly insurmountable.

It's been called possibility thinking, positivity, optimism and 'what can be.' Napoleon Hill, a contemporary of Ford's and author of the incredible book *Think and Grow Rich* said, "What the mind of man can conceive, it can achieve." It doesn't mean it will be easy or obvious, but it will always be possible.

It is almost guaranteed that the solution will lie outside your comfort zone. But the truth is, all growth happens at the edges of our comfort zones. Everything that's good that ever happened in your life was out of your comfort zone at some point.

I'm not asking you to jump way outside of it, but start with some baby steps. Stick your toe in the water and dare yourself to try something different. Open yourself to the possibility that the kid with the tattoos and the green hair has some really good ideas worth listening to. Open yourself to the radical notion that the thoughts that live so comfortably in your head just might be your biggest impediment.

The world doesn't look the same anymore. And isn't that great news?! Just as has been the case whenever the world has changed, there are more opportunities than problems. They just don't look like they used to. It's time to step up and decide that this exciting, strange new world is the one that you're going to conquer.

Helen Keller, another contemporary of Ford's and resident of an unimaginably challenging world, once said, "Security is mostly a superstition. Life is either a daring adventure or nothing."

Marketing lessons from the Kardashians

A bit of a 'heads up' about this one – it might make you a bit uncomfortable. Might even tick you off. Or maybe it will inspire you.   We'll see...

First, a passage from one of my favorite marketing gurus, Roy H. Williams, aka, The Wizard of Ads:

> "I have a theory about people who succeed: they cheat. And I'm in favor of it.
>
> I saw you recoil from that word a little, so I'll say it more delicately: they're quick to embrace an unfair advantage.
>
> Exceptional marketing gives a business an unfair advantage. Businesspeople who embrace this advantage are usually the ones who succeed.
>
> Here's why I call it "an unfair advantage": marketing doesn't improve the product or the service you provide but it can make a customer choose you anyway, even when your competitor is offering a better value.
>
> Your competitor's problem is that he doesn't know how to win attention and create a memorable impression. He's expecting his product to speak for itself.
>
> Products rarely do that."

Of course where Roy talks about products, the exact same rules apply to selling professional services. Far too many firms attempt to market themselves solely on the merits of who they are and what they do. This is what Roy refers to as letting a product speak for itself.

The problem with this approach is that you've got a whole whack of competitors who are every bit as good as you are. But when the dust has settled and you've all presented your qualifications, the game always ends in a draw. In that situation, a smart client has only one choice – select the firm with the lowest fee.

Exceptional marketing makes you stand out, even when what you're selling is pretty much the same as what your clients can get from your competitors. Think about it—the insurance policy you get from Geico is going to be virtually identical to the one you get from Progressive, or Farmers, or Allstate. But since Geico simply makes more noise than any of the rest of them, they dominate the market.

'Dominate'!? In 15 of the past 16 years, Geico has spent more on advertising than any of its competitors. Not coincidentally, in 15 of the last 16 years, Geico has grown in both revenue and market share.

And this is where we can learn some important marketing lessons from those oracles of wisdom, the Kardashians. These people aren't any smarter, better looking, nicer, sexier or better dressed than a million other people around the world. They're just better marketers.

They have mastered the use of public relations and social media in a way that most of us can't even dream of. As a result, these rather ordinary people have become famous for being famous. Oh, and built a reported combined net worth of $97 million, and climbing.

You can use the same tools to make the kind of noise in your chosen marketplace to achieve the results you want.

I regularly hear firms declare, "we will become the firm of choice in our market." Then they cross their fingers and hope. Yes, you can deliver competent, even remarkable service. But that's just the start.

If you fail to "win attention and create a memorable impression," in other words, if you merely let your services speak for themselves and fail to aggressively market, you're going to remain as one of many capable firms who wonder why they don't stand out in the crowd.

Whether or not you buy what the Kardashians are selling, they've figured out how to rise above a very crowded marketplace. And we'd all be wise to pay attention.

It's your money, why not ask for it?

The lawyers know something that most professionals either failed to learn or seem to forget: cash is a wonderful thing. And cash that's flowing in your direction can really make your day.

Not only do the lawyers know this, they do something to make sure that the cash is always flowing their way. They ask for – no, correct that – they insist on a retainer before they ever start working on your case. And if you've ever had occasion to hire a lawyer, you know that they're sticklers for keeping your cash in their pocket. Should your retainer balance fall too low, you're invited – no, correct that – commanded to top it up.

Why don't other professionals get a retainer? Because they never ask for it.

That's it. That's all there is to it. And you can be sure there aren't many clients out there volunteering to shove money into your hands before you've started the project. So it's entirely up to you to get the cash flowing.

Now I've been around the block enough to know that you might get some pushback on this issue. But that's simply negotiating. And sometimes negotiating means having to vigorously stand up for what's rightfully yours. The other day I heard from an architect who told me that his clients are regularly taking as much as 180 days to pay outstanding invoices. That's obscene to the point of being borderline criminal!

And yet it's all too common. Of course, once the work is done and the client has all your documents, you've got little in the way of leverage to apply in collections. Yes, you can file a lien, but many firms are reluctant to take that action and in some jurisdictions, the typical payment period is longer than the time in which you have to file one!

Insisting on a retainer, on the other hand, puts the leverage back in your hands. And it has little or no negative outcome for the client. Assuming they plan to pay you eventually, what difference does it make if they pay you now? Many clients have the cash in hand to pay for the project, so why not get it flowing your way earlier?

In these days of extremely tight fees, you can also use it as a bargaining tool. Since positive cash flow reduces your need to depend on a line of credit, you could offer to agree to the client's offer of a lower fee in exchange for getting a good portion of the money up front. Your cash is flowing and you don't have the hassle and stress of collections.

The remarkable thing is, in the rare situation when a firm asks for a retainer, as often as not the client agrees. We wring our hands and worry about poor cash flow and anticipate all kinds of pushback when, in fact, many if not most clients have no problem with it at all.

Why not give it a try? The worst that can happen is that they say, 'No!' and then you're in the same situation you are now. But my experience is that at least some of them are going to say, 'Sure, why not!' And your bank balance will be a lot higher and your stress level a lot lower.

Take your lawyer to lunch and have a chat about retainers. It'll be worth the price of the Chicken Caesar.

Oh, one more thing. For those clients who want to drag payment out until forever, NEVER offer a discount as an inducement for them to pay. If you discount the invoice, they'll see it as a reward to holding out so long and do it again the next time.

The most valuable book you can read

According to the United Nations Educational, Scientific and Cultural Organization (UNESCO), there were 304,912 new book titles published in the United States in 2013. That's alotta books! Among them were some truly fine works. Others, well...

But if you have any responsibility whatsoever for business development (and if you're reading this, you do) there is one book that I recommend to you above all others.

It wasn't published in 2013. It was first published in 1936 and has been in print, selling more than 15 million copies, ever since.

Written by a poor Missouri farm boy who had decided to make something better of himself, Dale Carnegie's *How to Win Friends and Influence People* has been guiding people who aim higher for almost 80 years.

It's 100% common sense, but the sort that we too easily and too often forget. For example, his "Six Ways to Make People Like You" are as obvious as botox on a Hollywood red carpet, yet how often do we forget to live by this timeless wisdom?

1. Become genuinely interested in other people.
2. Smile.
3. Remember that a person's name is, to that person, the sweetest and most important sound in any language.
4. Be a good listener. Encourage others to talk about themselves.
5. Talk in terms of the other person's interest.
6. Make the other person feel important – and do it sincerely.

Our profession provides daily opportunities to get crossways with clients, vendors, contractors, authorities and just about anybody else within earshot. But Carnegie offers such wonderfully farm-simple advice for avoiding, and then, if you have to, repairing the problems we have in dealing with others. We all should review his "Twelve Ways to Win People to Your Way of Thinking," every morning on the way to work.

1. The only way to get the best of an argument is to avoid it.
2. Show respect for the other person's opinions. Never say "You're Wrong."
3. If you're wrong, admit it quickly and emphatically.
4. Begin in a friendly way.
5. Start with questions to which the other person will answer yes.
6. Let the other person do a great deal of the talking.
7. Let the other person feel the idea is his or hers.
8. Try honestly to see things from the other person's point of view.
9. Be sympathetic with the other person's ideas and desires.
10. Appeal to the nobler motives.
11. Dramatize your ideas.
12. Throw down a challenge.

I've had a copy of this amazing book for years. But the other day, when I went to my library to refer to it, I discovered that someone has borrowed and neglected to return it. As I ordered another on Amazon I was actually quite happy to think that somebody else is also benefitting from this invaluable little tome.

If you've never read it or don't have your own copy, put down whatever you're doing, get one right away and have it read before another week goes by.

I've heard that Warren Buffett took the Dale Carnegie course (which is based on the book) when he was 20 years old. To this day, they say, the diploma is hanging in his office.

'Hope' is not a reliable marketing strategy

I encounter it regularly and it usually shows up in three varieties.

The first is the declaration that, "we will become the supplier of choice in our market." (

That's a nice, bold statement: "The supplier of choice." And wouldn't it be grand. Clients throughout your target market, in need of services, having dozens from which to choose, but setting them all aside in favor of a sole source selection of you!

It's actually possible. But it requires that you provide those clients with something that is simply unavailable from any other source. Something so valuable as to be worth whatever premium you might charge. And it requires that 'our market' know and be convinced about this thing that is so valuable.

And those are the bits that are invariably missing in whatever follows that "supplier of choice" statement. They never state where the value lies and they never say how they're going to get the word out to the market. Instead, they cross their fingers and hope.

The second is a firm or business unit or even an individual practitioner who submits more than 100 proposals in a year and has a sub-30% hit rate. I call this the 'fling-it-at-the-wall-and-hope-something-sticks' strategy. It's kind of like walking down the street, asking random strangers if they'd like to marry you. If someone is dumb enough to accept your rather off-hand proposal, the likelihood of happily-ever-after is pretty slim.

We've long since proven that a client who doesn't know you, hasn't worked with you before and yet still selects you from a large stack of proposals does not find loyalty and value to be worthwhile traits.

Finally, there is the CEO who confidently reassures me, "We rely on word-of-mouth for our marketing."

Did you ever play the 'telephone' game around a campfire when you were a kid? You know, the one in which you pass a message

25

around the circle and see what it's turned into by the time it comes back? Word-of-mouth is the marketing strategy in which you hope people say the right things about you and hope they say them often and loud enough to make an impact. It seldom works the way you'd hope.

In today's market, if you want to be the supplier of choice, you have to do something to make that happen. And delivering competent service isn't enough. Everybody does that. If you merely let your services speak for themselves and fail to aggressively market, you're going to remain as one of many capable suppliers who wonder why they don't stand out in the crowd.

Aggressive marketing is a mandatory function in today's business world. And successful marketing demands that you have a sophisticated understanding of and facility with its principles and applications. You don't design a bridge or treatment plant and hope that it works. You've learned how, you apply that knowledge and you are confident in the results.

Marketing is equally logical and hope has no place in it.

I hope it's sunny today and I hope I win the lottery. I have no control over either of those things so hope is the only strategy I can bring. But when it comes to the success of my business…

The worst possible way to spend your marketing money

I usually try to pass along best practices to you. You know, those things that the leaders consistently do that have us all admiring and looking up to them. But this week I'd like to shift my focus to the bottom rung and share a marketing tactic that is all too common, yet absolutely abysmal in its ability to convert your marketing dollars into sales.

And the all-time loser is…

Website banner ads.

Now maybe you knew this instinctively but there's some interesting science to back it up. There's even a term to describe it – 'banner blindness' – a phenomenon in web usability where visitors to a website consciously or subconsciously ignore banner-like information.

Perhaps 'ignore' is the wrong word. Turns out that readers don't really ignore banner ads so much as they actually don't see them at all. The ads are, for all intents and purposes, completely invisible to website visitors. They might just as well have a Star Trek cloaking device wrapped around them.

In some interesting research, test subjects were asked to search information on a website. During the experiments the subjects consistently overlooked both external ad banners and internal navigation banners. The placement of the banners on the page had little effect on whether or not they were noticed. Nor did it matter how big, colorful or animated the banners were. They were simply ignored.

To be fair, there is some other data that suggests they're not quite so invisible. But tests using eye-tracking scans show that the brutal truth of on-line behavior is that we simply don't see banners. It's not that we don't like them or wouldn't interact with them. We just don't see them.

So if you're thinking about paying for some banner ads to promote your firm, save yourself the trouble and simply set fire to your money instead. You can make them as big, beautiful and brilliant as you want. It won't matter. Because to a huge percentage of users, they are simply invisible.

Are you a devious, underhanded SOB?

Every competitive sport requires two levels of knowledge and skill for success. There are the basic, physical skills necessary to play the game well. A baseball player learns to throw and catch the ball. In basketball you learn to dribble and shoot.

Equally important is the strategic knowledge of the game: how to react in different situations, how to prepare a game plan to respond to the strengths and weaknesses of an opponent.

Since you're negotiating with clients, consultants and contractors all the time, a project manager or business developer has to master both sides of the negotiating game.

I'm a huge fan of win-win outcomes in every negotiation, but it's vital that you understand what win-win actually means. It's nice to imagine a scenario in which you and your client agree on every term, sing a verse or two of Kumbaya, and conclude with a group hug. Nice, and more than a little naïve.

Here's the deal—win-win does not mean you lie down and offer to be a doormat. There are plenty of clients out there who interpret 'win-win' to mean, "I win this and I win that too." Friendly, cooperative agreement on your part to any request your client makes does not result in both parties being treated fairly.

Win-win often means that you must vigorously defend what's rightfully yours. If your future client is also interested in achieving a fair outcome, the negotiation should be easy. But if they're out to win all the concessions they can, you must use your strength and your knowledge of negotiating tactics to win the concessions you need and defend against unreasonable demands.

In the game of chess, a gambit is a move for advantage. In the game of negotiating, it's the same thing. If you're going to become a skilled negotiator (and you must) it's vital that you learn, practice and master the tools of negotiation. Some of the tactics are well known. The 'Good-Cop, Bad-Cop' technique, for example, is an old favorite that appears in every detective movie. Others are less well known and subtler.

Many professionals, when they first learn these tactics, are offended by some of the seemingly 'low-down' tricks that can be (and are) regularly used in negotiating. I've met project managers who've decided that the tactics strike them as so underhanded that they can't imagine using them. But even if you never use The Flinch, The Nibble or The Red Herring, you'd better learn about them because they're being used on you all the time.

'Devious' (I've heard that word used) tactics like these might seem to be working against the goal of a win-win outcome. But you'd better realize that as much as you want both parties to walk away winners, your future client may not always share your sentiments. There's no shortage of clients who would like nothing better than to retain your services at the least possible price under terms and conditions that are decidedly in their favor.

A good negotiator understands that strength against strength will bring both parties to a successful and mutually agreeable conclusion. Taking the role of the doormat and agreeing to anything the other party asks for isn't win-win, it's volunteering to lose.

The politician and the goldfish

In the early months of 2009, Secretary of the Treasury Timothy Geithner was just a little preoccupied as the worst banking crisis since the Great Depression threatened to bring the financial system of the United States to its knees.

Later, when asked to describe his role, he said, **"It's like you're in the cockpit of the plane — your engine's burning, smoke's filling the cabin, it's filled with a bunch of people that are fighting with each other about who's responsible, you have terrorists on the plane and people want you to come out of the cockpit and put them in jail. And you have to land the plane. That terrifying core objective in a crisis is to make sure you first put out the fire."**

Mr. Geithner could have described the arcane financial wranglings and the backroom politics that must have been going on. But his choice of a metaphor to tell a story made that gut-wrenching time clear and understandable to those of us who were only standing by and hoping.

I frequently see professionals who are attempting to develop an 'elevator speech.' You know, that short, succinct description of what you do that can be told in the span of a 10-floor elevator ride. Most people make a huge mistake on their way to that quick, pithy description: They assume that the speech must magically, in 30 seconds or less, tell everything there is to know about your firm, your business or your career.

According to the National Center for Biotechnology Information, the average attention span of a human being has dropped from 12 seconds in 2000 to 8 seconds in 2013. Which, disturbingly, is one second less than the attention span of a goldfish.

Which is why politicians speak in sound bites.

Despite the stigma that has come to surround them, sound bites can be useful. They help people remember what you said and why you said it. When concise and colorful they reflect your personality and amplify your message. A great sound bite doesn't tell the whole story. It leaves the listener wanting to learn more. Which is exactly the outcome you want from your elevator speech. You want your listener to insist that you come back when she has more time.

The best elevator speech is a short story. And your business life is full of them.

"Our engineers helped Janine Jackson get to the hospital in 10 minutes along a road that used to be so congested it would have taken 30. It was a boy!"

"When Mayor Bigwig pledged that the new Little League ballpark would be open in time for the 4ᵗʰ of July celebrations, we helped him throw out the first pitch."

"We make sure that the western half of this state will always have an abundant supply of safe drinking water."

"PharmaCorp was committed to having the new drug line in full production before the end of the first quarter. Our firm had them ship a full month early."

Attention spans have never been shorter. You have never had more fascinating and compelling stories. Combine the two and you'll be an instant elevator hero.

The most wonderful thing you can do with PowerPoint

It will spin, twist and magically appear. It will directly insert online video clips, embed Flash animations and put flaming heads on the photos you've chosen. I wouldn't be surprised if the next release will remove those stubborn stains on your carpet.

But there is one thing that PowerPoint can do that is more powerful than any of these: It can turn off.

Right smack in the middle of your presentation, you can turn it off and talk, just talk to your audience. Amazing!

First let me show you how you do this. If you're running the program from a keyboard, press the 'B' key and the screen will turn black. Press the 'W' key and the screen will turn white. Press either key again and the slide you turned off is back on the screen. If you're using a remote, there's often a button that will turn off the slide.

Now let's talk about why you should use this feature.

The reason you're making a presentation is to connect with your audience. To engage with them in a way that gets them excited, persuades them, educates them or leaves them motivated to get up and do something different. If your purpose was merely to convey information, an email or a memo is probably a better idea.

No one has ever been excited, motivated or persuaded by simply watching PowerPoint slides click by. It takes a real live human being to engage an audience. Abraham Lincoln, JFK, Martin Luther King, Jr. and Winston Churchill never used PowerPoint, and likely wouldn't have even if it had been available. The best presenters, the best speakers, the best teachers and preachers know that the only way to connect with an audience is to engage them with eye contact, body language, vocal expression and genuine enthusiasm. None of those things can happen if we're all reading bullet points together.

Your slides are mostly decoration, augmentation and back-up to what you're saying. As long as they're up on the screen, the audience is distracted from the real presentation, which is you. Never forget that YOU, not your slides, are the presentation.

So, every once in a while, turn your slides off. Then tell a story, ask a question, invite comments from the audience and engage in some dialogue. They'll remember that long after they've forgotten your slide.

The logical, brilliant, simplicity of marketing

I used to be an architect. That was so hard! Non-stop and ever-changing rules, regulations, codes, budgets and schedules! I wasn't smart enough for that.

Marketing, on the other hand, is brilliantly simple. And that's the dirty little secret that marketers don't want you to know. There is nothing the least bit complicated about marketing. There are a few simple rules that, if you follow them, it works. And it works every time.

The flip side, though, is that if you DON'T know the rules, or if you only follow them occasionally, it doesn't work. You can pour all the time and money you've got into it and you'll get nothing but frustration.

Here's the deal: there are three simple rules of marketing. Follow them, and you win. Ignore them, you lose.

Rule #1: What makes you special?
What have you got that I can't get from every other firm? What can I get from you that isn't available on every street corner? What do you offer that nobody else can provide?
Sometimes it's a particular skill set. Do you offer capabilities that no one else can match? Do you solve problems that others can't? Can you turn projects around faster than anyone else?
Sometimes it's a process. Do you execute your projects in a unique way? Do you involve your clients? Do you have a way of working through the process that others envy?
Sometimes it's the way you treat your clients. In retail they call it the 'customer experience.'

Rule #2: What's in it for me?
Don't tell me that your firm was founded in 1958. Tell me that more than half a century of accumulated 'lessons-learned' will eliminate

potential mistakes and bring many time- and money-saving ideas to my project.

Don't tell me that you have an excellent track record of successful projects. Tell me that there will be fewer demands on my time, better decision-making, reduced risk and a much higher likelihood of on-time and on-budget delivery.

Rule #3: Over and over and over again.
Tell me once and I don't hear you. Tell me twice and I forget. Tell me twenty times and I begin to recall.

Do you ever wonder why Coca Cola, the world's best-known brand, continues to buy ad space? It's because they know they need to stay front and center in your mind if they hope to hang on to that precarious market position.

Your presence in the market is like that hole that forms when you stick your hand in a pail of water: pull it out and see how long it lasts.

Most firms equate marketing with proposal writing, the occasional trade show and a Tweet every six weeks whether they need it or not. And they wonder why they're treated like a commodity.

The rules of marketing are brilliantly simple. But like checkers, you have to know, and follow them if you hope to win.

It takes courage to be disruptive

L et's face it, the business world is not known for its revolutionaries. Nope, the practitioners here are pretty staid, conservative, law-abiding folks.

Not that there's anything wrong with staid and law-abiding. It just doesn't lend itself to revolution. And we could sure use one around here.

I'm now into my fifth decade in business. In the Architecture field, where I started, with the exception of reduced fees, increased liability and cutthroat competition, there isn't a whole lot that's changed. We still crank out drawings and specs, we still base our contracts on the same 'ol project phases (which didn't make sense then and make even less sense now) and we still go home after they've cut the ribbon, leaving the life-cycle revenue and value to somebody else.

I was around for the integration of CAD, in which we threw out the $300 drafting boards and replaced them with $3,000 workstations without leveraging the potential they offered.

And now we're bringing BIM into the mix.

Here's a truly revolutionary technology, with the potential to redefine how facilities are designed, built, managed through their life cycles and disposed of when we no longer need them. It offers design professionals the opportunity to stay involved with the facilities they design for years and years, adding value along the way and extracting profit from the revenue stream that flows from the ongoing operation of a built asset.

But the vast majority of firms are using it to produce a set of drawings. Period. Yes, we pull off some sexy renderings and fly-throughs, but hardly anyone is diving deep into the heart of this technology to dynamically model sustainability performance, real-time construction costs and sequencing, operational costs, and life-cycle asset maintenance and management. Almost nobody is positioning themselves to be the intelligence behind the infrastructure throughout its entire life.

Why not? Because that would be disruptive. And it takes courage to be disruptive.

What does being courageous actually feel like, and why is it so hard?

1. It takes vision.
You might see the ultimate potential of your venture. But it takes much longer for a) your vision to materialize, b) the rest of the world to see that vision, and c) the marketplace to demand it.

2. Everyone will fight you.
Almost everybody will doubt you and many will think you're just plain crazy. If you are really creating something new, most people won't believe it until they see it. And even then, they'll be skeptical of its market potential.

3. Obstacles are everywhere you look.
The road to disruption is full of technical, financial, mental and social challenges. It's extraordinarily difficult for an established company to disrupt itself. In addition to the normal chorus of doubters, you have to face your Board, employees, existing customers and partners.

We can stare all day long at the roadblocks and the obstacles. Then, at the end of that day, we haven't moved anywhere. Climbing a mountain is risky and hard. But the view from the top is spectacular.

How to get around the purchasing department

It's a common and growing trend – suppliers are routinely vetted and selected by Purchasing Departments instead of end users. And suppliers of services are not happy about it. I hear the complaints regularly: "The same people who are making buying decisions about office supplies are now evaluating complex professional services!"

The frustration is understandable. What's less clear is what to do about it. Here are some suggestions that will ease your frustration and, perhaps, help you beat them at their own game.

First, understand that you're not about to convince Mega Corp to change their purchasing policies. They've evolved to this process through some internal evaluation that seems to them to be the best idea right now. So stop banging your head against the wall. You're the only one getting a bruise on your forehead.

Second, rather than fight it, embrace their shift in procedure. After all, it's highly likely that there are enlightened, intelligent and open-minded people in Procurement who truly have their company's best interest at heart.

Once you've made these two mental shifts, follow the same procedures as you would if you were dealing directly with the Owner, the Facilities Department or whoever else you might prefer to be selling to.

1. Conduct a rigorous Go/No Go evaluation. If Purchasing truly is going to ignore the value you offer and immediately go to the bottom line, do you really want to work with this client?
2. Research the heck out of the Procurement Department. Who are the decision makers? What are their preferences and priorities? How do they think? What is their purchasing track record? What is the relationship between Procurement and

the Facilities Department?

3. Start building relationships with the people in Procurement. In the same way as you'd do business development activities with folks in Facilities, drop in to see the decision makers in Procurement. Put them on your content marketing distribution list. Invite them to your company events. Get to know them the way you've historically come to know your first-line clients.

4. Write your proposal knowing that the people in Procurement are going to evaluate it. Speak to their preferences. Address their hot buttons. Show and tell them what they want and need to see and hear. Make it easy for them to look good.

5. Don't assume that price is everything. (See note above about enlightened, intelligent and open-minded.) Procurement Departments understand the concept of value just like everyone else. Just make sure that you are fully informed on how they define and measure value and then hand it to them the way they want it.

6. If it turns out that price IS everything and you still want a piece of Mega Corp's work, learn a lesson from your Contractor friends and lowball the sucker. Then, after you've won the contract, tack additional services back on wherever you can. It's not immoral or unethical, it's how business is done.

It's time to accept that Procurement and Purchasing Departments are here to stay and stop pretending that the end user is going to over-ride them. It's time to learn how to play their game and win.

It ain't a goal if you're not moving toward it

What are you trying to make happen?

If you don't have dreams and hopes and aspirations you're probably no longer breathing. Part of the joy of being alive is our relentless reach to become or achieve something new, something larger, something better than what we are today.

What kind of progress are you making toward the goals you've set for yourself or your firm?

The first thing your goal needs to be is specific. You say you want your firm to grow. Great! How much? How fast? In what direction? If you can't paint me a really detailed picture of what things will look like once you've arrived, it's not a goal. It's a vague wish or even a fantasy.

Don't worry if your goal evolves. In fact, worry if it doesn't. Every step you take towards it gives you a different viewpoint, a different perspective on it. As you climb further up a mountain you learn more about it. Obstacles, shortcuts and breathtaking vistas come into view that weren't apparent from the bottom. The mountaintop doesn't change, but the way you get to it surely does.

The second thing about your goal is that you must be constantly moving towards it.

When you look back, can you see your own footprints in the ground you've already covered? Can you see and measure the forward progress you've made? Can you point to the actions you've taken that have moved you further along the path?

Or do you find yourself staring at the same scenery you were looking at last month?

Every worthwhile goal:

1. Has an action plan that drives it
2. Can measure the progress toward it
3. Will show up in daily action

Firm owner: Our goal is to become the firm of choice in our region.
Me: To what market?

Firm owner: Our goal is to open a new branch office this year.
Me: Tell me about the locations you've investigated so far.

Firm owner: Our goal is to grow by 15% this year.
Me: How does your year-to-date revenue compare with last year?

Project manager: My goal is to become a better presenter.
Me: Have you joined Toastmasters yet?

A goal that matters to you has to be touched every day, even if that touch is tiny – a note you scribble to yourself, a phone call, 10 minutes of research. If you're not taking action every day, it's not a goal. It might be a wish, a dream, a fantasy, but it's not a goal.

Dennis Waitley is a legendary speaker and change coach who talks about a wonderful, imaginary place called Someday Isle. You know, that place we'll all get to when the mortgage is paid, the kids have moved out and Rover has gone on to doggie heaven.

Someday I'll take that trip to Europe. Someday I'll write that novel. Someday I'll start my own company. Someday we'll improve our hit rate. Someday we'll update our website. Someday we'll get our marketing act together.

Can you see both the mountaintop ahead and your own recent footprints behind? Or are you living on Someday Isle?

Marketing 2.0

What kind of ideas do you allow into your head? Are they incremental or quantum?

Incremental ideas build on the past, taking the journey from A to B one step at a time. They are safe. They are predictable. They are rarely innovative or rebellious.

Quantum ideas, on the other hand, make an inexplicable leap to the next energy level. They redefine known realities and create previously unheard-of possibilities. They are risky. They are surprising. They give birth to revolution.

The marketing strategies that most firms use have their origins in the mid 1970s. They have evolved slowly over the past 40 years but haven't changed significantly. They're based on three fundamental tactics:

1. Building reputation through word of mouth
2. Fostering long-term, trust-based relationships
3. Responding to RFPs

Forty years ago (maybe even as recently as 15 years ago), these techniques served the profession well.

But the Great Recession, which began in December 2008, changed everything. The post-recession world is a dramatically different place and the game we're playing today is entirely different. The rules your Daddy played by won't win this game.

Why not?

If word-of-mouth is so reliable, how did that unknown firm from out of town sweep in and start stealing projects that used to belong to the locals? If relationships are so important, why is client loyalty disappearing? If responding to Requests For Proposals is such a terrific strategy, why are you consistently coming second?

Yes, there are firms that are doing well now. But when you peek behind the curtain, you learn that they've implemented a whole new set of strategies. They've adopted new ways of thinking about marketing and selling their services. And they're eating everybody's lunch.

When cautious people are in desperate need of revolution, the right answer comes in three steps:

1. Hang on to what's working and valuable
2. Toss out what's antiquated and ineffective
3. Adopt what's new and important

I get up every morning with the purpose of helping professionals across the country take those three steps. Help them understand and navigate the new landscape of marketing in this post-recession world. Help them win a steady supply of profitable work.

Real breakthroughs, the ones that change the game, can only come from a major shift in mindset. No matter how successful you already are, the jump to the next level can only take place if you allow yourself to have a different mindset. Because nothing advances until we advance how we think.

What kind of ideas do you allow into your head?

It's about time

I've had this query pop up several times in the last little while so I guess it's time to address the issue here.

"How much time should marketing staff spend to effectively market the firm outside of proposal and interview efforts?"

I'm going to go with the classic, "that depends" kind of answer.

In a stable environment, that is to say, you're not trying to grow into a new market or geography or haven't recently acquired a firm and are trying to communicate that brand shift, it should be about 60/40 in favor of proposals and interviews.

Now, that's not how I'd like it to be in my perfect world. But the reality is that most firms build their marketing strategy around responding to RFPs so 60/40 is what it takes under that premise.

It's my firm belief, however, that there should be much more emphasis on brand building, eventually reversing that split so more time is spent on building your brand. There's no doubt that every hour you spend reinforcing and strengthening your brand, you make it easier to sell individual projects.

In my ideal world, 80% of your effort would be on branding, business development and relationship building and just 20% on proposal writing, most of which would be simple confirmation letters.

But, alas, many professionals haven't yet bought into the incredible power of brand so they keep throwing proposals at the wall and hoping that something sticks.

Now back to the 'that depends'. Let's say you're expanding into a new market or geography or you're launching a new service. In this case you need, more than anything, to build name recognition, get some buzz going about the firm and let the decision makers in this new market know you've arrived. You'll want to devote almost all your effort to building your brand for the first six months or so.

Email marketing, heavy social media, some well-coordinated

public relations, maybe an article or news feature or two is what you want. Chasing RFPs at this point is going to get you a whole lotta nuthin. You're the new kid in town and you have to strut your stuff before anybody's going to give you the time of day. Don't waste your time writing proposals – you're not going to win anything. And even if you do, it will be for all the wrong reasons.

There's another version of the question that I heard just last week:

"What percentage of time should a classic seller/doer be spending on business development activities?"

If it's a Project Manager who is responsible for a team, he or she should spend at least 20% of their time – one full day per week – out there glad-handing, schmoozing and closing on projects. And as you gasp, note that I said, "at least."

If we're not selling, then everything is overhead. "Sellers" are a lot harder to find than "Doers" and hence more valuable. Want to be invaluable to your firm? Get out there and sell.

You can't sell it if you don't understand it

More than a decade ago I was asked to be the VP of Sales and Marketing at a good-sized construction company. When I stepped into the job I inherited a marketing staff of seven.

It was a talented group. Impressive writers, graphic designers, editors and marketing theorists, but…

One afternoon, the lead proposal writer came into my office and asked, in a sincere and completely un-ironic way, "What is design-build?"

With my jaw on the floor I realized that, as great as this team was at marketing, they had no idea what we were selling.

The company had seven Divisions including hospitals, industrial plants, retail developments, airports and interior fit-ups, all depending on my team to show them in the best possible light. How could I expect the head of the healthcare group to trust one of my team to write a great proposal for the next hospital project if they didn't even understand a simple construction concept like design-build?

The next morning I outfitted the entire team with hard hats and work boots and we started our construction education. We made regular visits to the job sites, sat in on job meetings and bought the donuts and coffee for the weekly Superintendent's meeting. We watched pile driving, concrete pours and sheet rock installation. They learned about subcontractor coordination and the life-and-death importance of controlling dust when you're renovating a neo-natal intensive care unit.

In short, they got their boots dirty and their eyes full of exactly what the company got paid to do and what they were helping to sell.

The immersion course lasted for about a month, but the education didn't stop there. Although we backed off a bit from the initial intensity, we maintained weekly site visits and regular conversations with the estimating and preconstruction teams.

The results were as staggering as the initial shock had been. Their level of understanding of the content of the proposals they were writing shot up and it allowed them to communicate the value the company provide far more compellingly. They had a whole new facility with the language of construction and our hit rate went up.

But the biggest benefit was the new level of communication between the technical folks and the marketing team. They'd won some admirers when they showed up for the 5AM meetings in their work boots and the job-hardened construction pros gave them a whole new level of respect.

Don't misinterpret. This does NOT mean that everyone on your marketing team ought to be engineers, architects or otherwise have some technical background. I get that reaction frequently when the technical folks roll their eyes if the new Head of Marketing didn't come with a P.E. or AIA after their name.

In fact, I often shy away from the technical-professional-turned-marketer because they frequently don't have the communication skills that are necessary. Tough as this may sound, it's usually a lot easier to teach a marketer enough about design or construction than to teach a technical professional how to communicate persuasively.

How much does your marketing team know about what your firm does? How often are they out at a job site? Have they ever sat through a tough project management meeting and seen what goes on? Can they talk the talk?

You can't sell what you don't understand.

Do your business developers have the 'sales gene'?

WARNING!
This blog post contains course language including words such as 'sales,' 'selling' and 'quotas' that may not be suitable for some professionals.

I regularly hear that Business Developers and Seller-Doers are not living up to expectations in the Sales department. You could try sales training, but it's a waste of time and money if those you're training don't have the 'Sales Gene.'

The Sales Gene is a combination of three core personality traits that all successful salespeople share:

- Need for Achievement
- Competitiveness
- Optimism

Collectively, we refer to them as 'Drive.'

Most classic rainmakers, or 'hunters,' score high in all three of these traits. If any one is missing, that person's success as a business developer is sketchy. They can contribute as part of a team or by nurturing existing clients, but they're simply not going to make it as a steady producer when it comes to landing new work.

More than 80 years of research and experience prove that Drive can't be taught. You're born with it, or you're not. How can you know if your business developers have it?

It's too easy to talk about 'introvert' and 'extrovert.' That basic personality assessment isn't nearly fine-grained enough to help. And without a more sophisticated assessment, the Sales Gene can be nearly impossible to identify.

As nice as it would be to hire nothing but High Drive personalities who are itching to get out and sell, the reality of your team is different and you need to make the most of what you've got.

Using sliding scales of Achievement, Competitiveness and Optimism there are four sales types:

The **Collaborator** is focused on a good work-life balance. They can make effective business development contributions, but only when paired with a highly driven 'hunter' or asked to manage existing client accounts.

The **Believer** is strongly optimistic, which helps overcome the rejection that others can't handle. These salespeople can help maintain the team's morale but may not be able to sustain enough Drive to convert high hopes to closed sales on their own.

The **Realist** is an achievement-oriented, competitive individual with medium to low optimism. These salespeople generally need encouragement through mentoring or being teamed with high optimism partners.

The **Driver** is strong in all three traits. They have the motivation and resiliency that's needed for success in 'intense account acquisition roles,' which is Psychologist-speak for selling.

It would be wonderful if each of your Business Developers and Seller-Doers were blessed with that driven, 'hunter' instinct. But they're not. And coaxing, bribing, cajoling and threatening them isn't going to change anything. Perhaps it's time to be a little more fine-tuned in your staff assessments, your responsibility assignments and your expectations.

Are you paid, earned or owned?

Under the broad umbrella of 'marketing' lies one of the important sub-species we call PR or Public Relations. Often, the only nod to PR is to send out the occasional press release that, mysteriously, never seems to make it into the press. More on that in a minute.

If you're going to adopt PR as part of your marketing strategy, it helps to have a more in-depth understanding of what it entails.

First, let's change the term to 'Media Relations' because not only is 'the press' just one of numerous media outlets, it's the one that's in a precipitous decline. Traditional print newspapers and magazines are an endangered species and online media is taking over. And with the explosion of online channels, your options for a media strategy have exploded too.

Regardless of the media channel, there are three very different approaches you can have towards your media exposure – paid, earned and owned.

Paid media is when you pay to have a presence in someone else's media channel. Traditionally this is when you buy advertising in a newspaper, magazine or website. Within the limits of the media outlet's rules, you decide what you want to say in the ads you place and cross your fingers that someone who matters will read it and respond.

Earned media is when someone who's in charge of their own media outlet decides to write about you, share your content, speak about your brand and otherwise talk about you. The mentions are 'earned,' because they are voluntarily given by others who feel you deserve it. Historically, earned coverage happened when a traditional media outlet such as radio, TV or the press chose to cover some aspect of your firm, either a profile of a Principal or a completed project. Today it can still include that, but it can also mean clients, friends or colleagues who forward, retweet or otherwise pass along the content you've created.

Owned media is when you make use of a channel you create and control. This could be your company blog, YouTube channel, your website, or even your Facebook page. Even though you don't strictly 'own' your YouTube channel or Facebook page, you control the content and don't have to pay for usage.

As you can imagine, the credibility that any reader gives to the content will vary depending on whether it's paid, earned or owned. While advertising can be effective, we're far more skeptical about its content than if we read the same thing in an article published by a third party. That's the reason your press release rarely makes it into print. The Editor or News Director decides if their readers or viewers will be sufficiently interested in the item before they run it. If it's a totally self-serving piece that's only of interest to you, it will end up in the round file.

Media Relations should never be seen as a source of winning new projects. The likelihood that someone is going to see your ad, the article about you or watch your YouTube channel and decide to award you their next project is slim to none. Using it should be part of your overall branding strategy, working to build name recognition and enhance your reputation, rather than to sell projects.

Next week, we're going to be out of business

No, not us!

But I heard this phrase spoken by a senior executive recently and he meant it literally. The backlog for his particular group had shrunk so much that, if they didn't find some new projects within the next seven days, everyone in the department would have to go.

This, in the middle of an economic boom!

Like the paramedics in the emergency department, let's stop the bleeding first. Later we'll figure out what happened and what we need to do about it.

If you find yourself in a tight corner, it's time for desperate measures. Here's what to do:

- Make a limited time offer. Send an email out to every client you've ever worked for and let them know that, for the next 30 days only, they can buy your talent for 25% off the normal rates. But they have to act fast.
- Create your own projects. Brainstorm every client you've served and every project you've set foot on for the past two years and make a list of all the 'didn't-have-time-for,' and the 'one-day-we'll-get-around-to' projects that every client has. Develop a scope of work and a lump sum price that's heavily discounted, then offer it, unsolicited, to the client.
- Phone everyone you know, including your competitors, and ask if they need help. This isn't the time to be too proud.
- Visit with people at other places that you know to be busy and offer your team as overflow support. Offer to discount your rates so they make a small margin on your work.

The goal is to get some cash flowing – fast. And it's not going to happen if you sit around waiting for the phone to ring.

As soon as the victim is stabilized, it's time to address the bigger question: "What happened!?"

The short answer is that the market has forgotten about you. The number of clients you've been working for has shrunk below that critical mass needed to sustain itself. When there are only a handful of clients, it's inevitable that they're going to run out of things for you to do.

I see it way too often – you are so focused on doing projects that you forget to look up and notice that your client list is shrinking and your competitors are circling.

The recession created a huge number of new competitors in many industries. A large percentage of the professionals who were laid off had no choice but to hang out their own shingle and start competing with you. And usually at much lower rates because the spare bedroom is a much smaller overhead burden than your office space.

When the recession ended, there was such a huge, pent-up demand that many firms forgot to do their longer-term marketing. The branding and relationship-building that ensure there is always a buzz out there about you were set aside. Clients have so many choices today so when you pulled your hand out of the pail of water, the hole it made disappeared instantly.

There are only three things necessary to running a successful business – Get work. Do work. Keep score. Notice which one comes first! No matter how good the economy is, you can never take your eye off the marketing ball. What are you doing to win work in the next 30 days? Six months? Two years?

Make one point, and make it well

Good marketing makes a single point, powerfully. Bad marketing sounds like a grocery list.

We shoot ourselves in the foot when we try to sell everything at once. Whether it's a business development meeting, a casual lunch or a sales presentation, we feel compelled to dump everything and the kitchen sink on them at once. "We do this, we do that, we've done the other thing… Oh, and if you'd like, we can do that too!"

The urge is understandable. You want them to know everything you do, because they're sure to have a long list of needs. Now, it might seem counter-intuitive, but the less you try to communicate, the more likely it is that they'll listen and respond. Focused and succinct beats out complex and vague every day of the week.

At any given moment, most clients have one dominant priority, one issue that's top-of-mind. It changes from day to day, and even moment to moment, but there will always be one thing that's more important than all the others. Your task is to figure out what this particular moment's crisis is, and be the solution.

How do you discover their priorities? You listen. You stop talking and you listen. As long as you're talking, you learn nothing. But shut up for a moment and you'll hear everything that's on their mind. The best sales people learn early that selling is about listening, not talking.

If the Mayor of Podunk is in the news – again – because lower Main Street is flooded again, she doesn't want to hear about the great waste treatment plants you design. But tell a couple of stories about your successes in storm water management and she'll want to talk with you all day.

Your entrée to a client is like one of those wall anchors you buy at Home Depot. It pierces the wallboard with a very narrow, sharp point. Once inside, it expands to a width that'll hold up a 50-pound bookshelf forever.

Your job is to get a foot in the door. Once inside, there'll be plenty of time and opportunity to look around, see what else needs to be done, have great conversations about all the additional services you offer and settle in for the long haul.

Resist the urge to tell them everything. It's a whole lot easier to get in the door with a narrow, focused and timely message than it is with a long grocery list of options.

The most important trait for any business developer

Business development is unlike any other job_because the rejection is non-stop. The constant stream of invalidation that salespeople experience is a natural part of the job. But it's also a bear to handle. Rejection affects the way a person feels about him or herself and can breed emotions of shame, resentment, guilt and low self-worth.

Successful business developers, on the other hand, look at rejection differently.

Most importantly, they bring an unyielding send of optimism. These people face rejection frequently, and yet they still persevere. They don't take it personally. They don't dwell on it. And they are absolutely certain that their next call will surely be successful.

I can hear the pessimists from here: "We're not pessimistic, we're realistic!" "That optimist simply refuses to face reality."

Perhaps. But the fact remains that business developers who are innately optimistic are more successful. It's that simple.

Why?

The pessimistic business developer starts to lose motivation quickly after a few rejections. She often sees sales leads as futile if they don't show immediate signs of interest or there's the slightest hint of resistance or competition. This can lead her to avoiding new leads or heading into the sale with the self-fulfilling attitude that "it's not going to work regardless".

It would be wonderful if there were an 'Optimism Pill' or if the sales trainer or motivational speaker could truly effect real change. But the fact is that optimism is an inherent trait. You're born with it and nurture it in your early years. Or not. By the time you're heading down your career path, you either have it or you don't.

Research overwhelmingly shows that without built-in optimism, you have very little chance of becoming a high-performing business developer. The rejection quotient is just too tough to handle over time.

It's kind of like baseball. You can be struck out three out of every four times at bat, and still be at the top of the game. For sales people and business developers, the ratio is much worse – more like one in 10. So the upbeat attitude and optimism to roll with those other nine punches is absolutely critical.

If you're wondering why your seller-doers are *doing* a lot more than they're *selling*, you might want to look at their innate levels of optimism. If that key ingredient is missing, or the levels are low, the chances of success are pretty slim.

Granted, that person might have been pretty impressive when you first met. Optimism is pretty easy to fake in a few conversations. But over the long haul, and especially when there is a real expectation and need for them to bring in work, the lack of optimism is impossible to hide.

Falling short on optimism does not mean that you've failed. In fact, there's a very real advantage working with someone who brings a healthy dose of skepticism and assumes things are going to fail. Bridges and buildings designed by these folks tend to stay up no matter what.

But if you want someone who's going to sell for you, bring along the Optimist.

I'm the only one who can do this

I learned a big lesson earlier today.

A very important colleague produced some work that was absolutely fabulous. On every level it was accurate, high quality and completely in support of what we do here. The only problem was, it wasn't the way I would have done it.

So I concluded that it was wrong.

And I told him so.

In one inspired move I managed to accomplish several things:

- Create a rift between myself and this valuable team member
- Miss out on an important contribution
- Limit our ability to grow
- Undermine this talented and intelligent person's confidence

It's so easy to be seduced by our own talents. And I see many leaders make the mistake of associating with people just like themselves. You've likely been there. You meet someone there are some really strong, positive vibes. In fact, this person even reminds you a bit of yourself. He or she has many of the same characteristics as you do, even the same quirky sense of humor.

What's not to like?

Insisting that everyone around you look, think and act like you is dangerous on many levels. First, when a candidate reminds you of yourself, you're often blind to their negative traits. Your doppelganger shares your shortcomings too.

Second, you have one point of view. It's not the only one. And it's not always the right one. Surrounding yourself with talented people who may not always agree with you forces you to stay flexible and open to new ideas. Mostly it forces you to continue to grow.

I frequently see firms in which it's apparent that the original founder hired employee number two to look like the person they see in the mirror. And on it went. Like the shallow end of the gene pool, those firms become rigid and lack the ability to adapt to the world as it changes around them.

I'd thought I was smarter than that. Apparently not.

I've got some work to do now. There's some crow to be eaten, a relationship to repair and a mind to be made more flexible. This might take a while.

In the meantime, I suggest you, too, look in the mirror. If everyone around you looks, acts and thinks like you, it might be time to consider what you're missing.

Brainstorming on glass

I regularly find myself facilitating a brainstorming session. Often it's for strategic planning, sometimes it's to develop a win strategy for an important project. The purpose doesn't matter.

Critical to the brainstorming process is a big place to write, capture ideas, draw big arrows to connect them, make little diagrams, doodle and generally free your mind to engage in some really creative thinking. Flip charts are okay, but they're small. White boards are okay too, but they fill up too fast. SmartBoards are fun, but not everybody has one.

The worst part of a small writing surface is that it cramps us. We feel obliged to save those precious few square inches for only the best ideas. That squashes all kinds of creativity because we never know what the best ideas are going to be until we've collected a bunch from which to choose.

The absolute biggest, baddest and best brain-storming medium I've ever found is the plate glass windows that surround so many boardrooms.

If your office or boardroom has big, expansive windows, or glass walls between you and the hallway, you're in luck. Window glass acts just like a dry-erase board. Just a whole lot bigger! And when you're busy writing and doodling all over the windows, there's a little bit of 'bad boy' in me who gets let loose and frees up the creative spirits. Bad boys and girls come up with all manner of off-the-wall ideas.

I've brainstormed on so many windows over my career that I've lost count. We've filled entire window walls with notes. Wall-to-wall, floor-to-ceiling. It's a mess when we're done. But wow, are we ever creative!

You know what's really fun, though? It's when you're working away with the project team, making great progress and the CEO walks in to see how things are going. More often than not they'll pause, look at the doodling all over their precious glass, start to ask, then stop, scratch their head, and walk back out without saying a word. It's quite entertaining.

So write on the glass. Go nuts. Free your inner thinker and let the ideas flow.

Just remember to use the dry erase markers.

Five steps to proposal success

Some interesting statistics for you to ponder:

- There are about 260 work days in a year.
- The average firm submits about 125 proposals during those 260 days. That's about one every other day.
- Even in the lower quartile of the statistics, firms submit about 55 proposals each year, which is more than one a week.
- At the upper quartile, firms are submitting more than 300 proposals annually, which, near as I can figure, is about one every six hours.

OMG!

A few weeks back I was helping a firm build a more effective brand-building plan. (In part, so they wouldn't have to write so many proposals!) One of the skeptics in the group complained that the firm seemed to be transitioning from an engineering firm to a marketing company. Even if you're doing a proposal a week, that's probably more than your total projects, which makes your firm a proposal-writing company!

I get it that responding to RFPs is one of the most important methods of winning work and sometimes it's not an activity that can be avoided. But there are two basic approaches to it:

- Throw a bunch at the wall and assume that something will eventually stick; or
- Make your proposals the best they can possibly be and make sure they stick

If you subscribe to the numbers game approach, your Marketing Coordinators have my deepest sympathy. Please provide them with plenty of really good coffee and be prepared for high turnover.

But if you'd rather take the high road, targeting only the best project opportunities and laser-targeting your proposal responses, there are five key elements that will help drive up your hit rate.

1. Use a strictly enforced go/no review process. Make it much harder to say 'yes' than 'no.' Make Managers accountable for their hit rates. Become more exclusive rather than more general.

2. Having given a proposal the green light, develop a detailed win strategy for each project chase. The days of 'Save As' are long gone and clients have to see a proposal that's been developed uniquely for them if you want to make the short list.

3. Make a smack-me-between-the-eyes first impression. Clients don't have time to review every proposal they get, cover-to-cover. In most cases they'll give it a cursory skim and decide if it warrants further attention. You've got less than a minute to make your case.

4. Make it all about the client. Don't tell them the history of your firm, tell them what you're going to do for them, how easy it's going to be to work with you and how wonderful life is going to be once they've made the decision to select you.

5. Tell stories. The vast majority of proposals are a collection of lists. Long, boring, one's-the-same-as-the-next lists. Lists suck the life out of a project. But stories relate how hard you worked, how you developed that game-changing idea, how you went the extra mile.

You are obliged to write proposals. But your client is under no obligation whatsoever to read them. Use these five steps to ensure that every proposal you write puts you at the very top of the short list.

The project report card

The first day of school, whether it's the first day of class in 4th grade arithmetic or post-graduate paleoanthropology, is about expectations. The teacher will always tell the students what will be expected of them and how their performance will be evaluated. You remember: "20% of your mark will be on class participation, 40% on your term paper and 40% on the final exam."

The point was that, from the very first day, you knew exactly what you had to do and how you were going to be evaluated.

As the semester went along, you'd get mid-term reports – periodic evaluations of your progress to date and a chance to pull up your socks if things weren't looking too good. Then, at the end of the year, after numerous opportunities for feedback, you'd get a final report card.

Protest as we might, no one could ever claim to be blindsided by that 'F.' You had plenty of notice and plenty of opportunity to do something about it.

Many professionals want to get feedback from their clients. They want to know they're measuring up when it comes to service, quality, responsiveness and who knows how many other metrics. But there are two serious flaws in the process that most people use.

1. They never ask, at the beginning of the project, what the client is going to be expecting and how they'll be evaluated.
2. They wait until the end of the project, when it's too late to make any adjustments, to get the one and only report card.

Sorry, kid. You failed. Better luck next time.

Most firms make assumptions about what the client wants and how they'll score the firm's performance. Sometimes they're right. Frequently they're not.

Wouldn't it be so much easier to sit down with each client,

before the project has even begun, to talk about expectations and evaluations? Wouldn't take long, but I know there are a whole lot of clients out there who would think it's a fantastic way to kick off a project.

Then, once you've established the expectations and evaluation criteria, wouldn't it make sense to seek out interim reports based on the criteria that had been set up? To see how you're doing while there's still time to make adjustments?

Projects have many natural milestones. Invoicing, cost estimating and other reviews take advantage of them all the time. Why not institute a quick performance evaluation at those same markers? It wouldn't be hard – just a quick rundown of the priorities you'd set up with the client at the start. Not only would your team have the chance to pull up its socks, your client is bound to be impressed by your proactive approach.

I hear firms tell their clients, "We'll exceed your expectations," almost daily. But rarely do those firms put anything behind that statement. Here's your chance to show your clients that you really mean it. And, like students in the school year, give yourself the opportunity to improve your marks along the way.

Project manager sales tips

Project Managers carry a big load. Plan the project, build the schedule, manage the budget, keep the client happy, herd the cats… Oh, and while you're at it, sell more work please!

When it comes to selling more work, the PMs are in one of the best positions to do that regularly. But it takes a bit of focus and a regular reminder to include business development on the daily agenda. Here are some suggestions that will help Project Managers make a major contribution to the 'get work' process without having to sacrifice billable time.

- Be constantly on the lookout for opportunities with the clients you're serving. It's way too easy to get wrapped up in the scope of the current project and miss the other developments within the client's company or agency. Walk around a bit. Observe what's going on. Ask questions about their long-term goals and try to meet other people within the client's organization who might know about other initiatives.
- Make sure you're fully versed on all the services your firm offers and look for opportunities to bring those services into a client's operation. Too often, a PM in the Civil Engineering Department forgets that the firm also offers Architectural Design (or vice versa). And just as often, we hear clients say, "I didn't know you offered that!"
- When you're in conversation with the client, learn about her network of colleagues. Find out what they do and which consultants they use. Let her know that you'd appreciate an introduction and a recommendation. If you've been treating the client well, they're usually happy to help you build your business.
- Always be on the lookout for additional scope opportunities within the current project. And when you see them, don't be afraid to identify them as such! Too many professionals equate

additional scope items as 'nickel-and-diming' the client and are reluctant to ask for extra fees. If the client pushes back, remind yourself that they're just negotiating. If they can get you to do it for free, why wouldn't they try?

- Set yourself a quota for sharing a meal with clients, contractors, decision makers and other network connections. Two per month is entirely reasonable for a Project Manager.
- Add one additional item to every project meeting agenda: "Mr./Ms. Client, is there anything else we can be doing for you, helping you with, or looking at for you at this time?"

Project Managers have a lot on their plates, to be sure. But business development is one of the most important responsibilities and these easy ideas can help your contribution to winning work go way up.

Why do we need marketing?

Why do we need marketing?

Believe it or not, I hear this question regularly. Not so much these days, when the economy is chugging along quite nicely, and we're not as frantic about overheads. But just wait till things tighten up a bit and watch out!

It's a legitimate question, though. Marketing isn't the core of what you do. Clients don't pay you to market to them. And, as we've discussed in previous blogs and webinars, it's even hard to accurately measure the ROI it provides.

Many firms believe that their work should stand for itself and anyone who cares to look would instantly know that the choice is obvious. Oh, if only it were so simple!

The problem with letting your work stand for itself is that you've got competitors, sometimes dozens of them, whose work stands just as tall, proud and exemplary as yours. We need marketing to communicate those things that truly set you apart from all those competitors. To show the unique specialness that is only you.

One of my favorite marketing gurus is Seth Godin. If you're not following him and reading his books and blogs, it's way past time that you did. Find him at sethgodin.com and learn to think about marketing in a way that you've likely never done before.

He recently summed up the challenge of marketing by posing a set of seven questions. See if you can answer them quickly, uniquely and meaningfully. That means, in a way that is vastly different than your competitor would and in a way that resonates in the heart.

1. Who are you trying to reach? If you answer, 'Everyone,' start over. It's neither possible nor desirable to be in love with everyone.
2. How will they become aware of what you have to offer?
3. What story are you telling? Are you and everyone associated

      with you consistently living and demonstrating that story every day?

4.   Does the story you're telling resonate with the views and attitudes and prejudices of these people? (Do they believe you? Does it get them excited?)

5.   Where is the fear that prevents them from taking the action you'd like them to take? Why do they hesitate?

6.   When do you expect these people to take action? If your answer is, 'Now', what prevents them from saying, 'Later'? It's much safer to delay.

7.   What are these people telling their friends about you?

Marketing is the way in which you connect and converse with both the customers you have and those that have yet to become customers. It's the way you bond so that the story you're telling resonates with them. It's the way they build up a strong preference for working with you when the opportunity arises. It's the way they come to like you, to trust you and to depend on you.

We need marketing for the same reasons a good marriage needs conversation. That's how it begins. That's how it's sustained.

Marketing vs. business development

I'm asked about it all the time and I overhear it in conversations too: "Which is more important – marketing or business development?" The fact that the question is asked at all shows that the person or firm doing the asking doesn't understand the respective roles of the two and is missing out on a huge opportunity to make selling services a whole lot easier.

Let's look at the vastly different roles that these vital first and second steps in the sales process play.

The objective of marketing (I'd prefer to call it 'brand building') is NOT to win projects. Now before you dismiss it out of hand, you should realize that there are some important things that need to be done before you can ever sell a project. The role of branding building is to 1) build name recognition, 2) enhance your reputation and 3) build what marketers call 'Mind Share.'

Put a different way, brand building is where you 1) let your target market know your firm exists, 2) educate them about how great their world will be when they work with you and 3) repeat 1 and 2 often enough that your entire target market is thoroughly familiar with your firm whether they've worked with you or not.

Imagine how hard it would be to sell upscale cars, running shoes or discount car insurance if no one had ever heard of 'The ultimate driving machine,' 'Just do it!,' or '15 minutes will save you 15%.'

Business development, on the other hand, is the second vital step in the sales process. Once a prospect knows about your firm, they need to develop a trust-based relationship before they're ready to commit. Business development is where you establish and proactively maintain those one-to-one, personal relationships that lead to doing business together. Lunches together, a little golf, maybe a baseball game now and then… It's the one-on-one time together that makes business development work.

Brand building uses tools like public relations, social media, advertising, etc. to talk to your whole market simultaneously. The cost-per-touch is low, but so is the level of personal connection. Business development can only deal with one prospect at a time. It's more time consuming and expensive, but it builds that all-important relationship.

Brand building goes nowhere if it's not followed up with proactive business development. Business development is REALLY DIFFICULT if you haven't prepped the market with an effective branding effort.

Let me ask you this: "Which is more important – your arm or your leg?" My guess is that you'd rather hang on to both as they each perform different and yet pretty important functions. Same goes for marketing and business development. The answer is, "Both!"

Ya gotta poke the sleeping dog occasionally

The other day a friend told me that I am 'deliberately disruptive.' I took it as a compliment.

I actually work quite hard to be as disruptive, unsettling and thought provoking as possible. Why? Because the design professions are like that frog in the pot of water where someone keeps turning up the heat. We're quietly going to boil to death if someone doesn't jump soon.

You want an example of head-in-the-sand? I was having a conversation recently with an architect who was bemoaning the growing popularity of design-build among their clients. Design-build!? That horse left the barn ages ago and we might as well be upset that cars are taking over the roads!

The building industry is about as mature and set in its ways as it gets. Let's face it, the Assyrians were building roads, bridges, water systems, and elaborate buildings too. We're just carrying on with a very long tradition. Our tools are more sophisticated (and expensive!) but our methods of doing business haven't evolved very far.

Without new business models, updated means of differentiating ourselves, and progressive ways of marketing we're going to become like those Assyrian museum pieces. Interesting, but irrelevant.

Back in the mid-70s when I first started in this business, it was considered unethical to publish even a business card as an advertisement. You could get called in and your knuckles rapped for such unprofessional conduct. Today we're in a knock-'em down, drag-it-out fight over pennies as we cooperate with our clients to drive the industry further and further into commodity status. Somebody has to pull the rug out from underneath us if we're to survive and thrive into the future.

I remember way back in architecture school when they told us that if we just did our work well enough, everything would take care of itself. It was a barefaced lie. Doing your work well is the barest minimum requirement to get you in the game.

It's my intention to call out that lie, rattle our comfortable cages and sweet-talk, scare, bribe, cajole and otherwise persuade you in any way I can to think about a different way to market and sell your design services.

Cuz I'm really not that into boiled frog.

Five reasons why clients won't hire you

You have a great firm. You do great work. You have great people working for you.

And yet, unless your hit rate is 100% there are prospective clients out there who choose not to buy what you sell. What's wrong with them?!

Turns out, they're no different than you, me and every other human being on the face of the planet. We all have five big reasons why we choose not to buy at any given moment. Doesn't matter if it's shoes, a new car or professional services, these five reasons are at play all the time. If you're a business developer who wants to turn prospects into clients, you need to pay attention to them.

1. They perceive that they don't need what you're selling.

It's been a long time since we bought only what we need. In fact, most of the buying we do is for things we desire far more than things we need. Your clients are the same – they don't NEED what you sell, but they WANT the benefits it brings. As a business developer, it's your job to connect those powerful desires directly to the services you provide.

2. They don't have any money to pay for what you're selling.

Funny thing about money – unless one is truly destitute, we always seem to be able to pay for the things we perceive to be really important. The fact is people buy what they want if they want it more than they want the money it costs. As a business developer, it's your job to show how the benefits you provide are more valuable than the money they cost.

3. They're just not in a hurry.

If your house in on fire, you're in a hurry for the fire department. Otherwise, most things can wait till tomorrow, till next week or forever. The status quo is a pretty comfortable place and it requires effort to move off that spot. There's an old saying: "The best time to plant a tree is 20 years ago. The second best time is right now." As a business developer, it's your job to let them see that there's no time like the present.

4.   They don't really want what you're selling.
No one ever saves up to hire the engineer or the architect. And clients really don't want to hire you. They DO want the results of what you do – clean water, commodious buildings, efficient transportation – but you're a necessary evil on the way to those benefits. As a business developer, it's NOT your job to sell them your services. It's your job to sell them the wonderful life they'll have as a result.

5.   They don't trust you.
No prospective client will ever come out and say, "I don't trust you." But they've had promises made and broken so many times by people that talked just like you… "We'll get it done on time!" Nope. "We'll get it done within your budget!" Nope. "We put our clients first!" Nope, again.

Trust takes a long time to build. It doesn't come with your website, your brochure or your proposal. It only comes from your actions. As a business developer, it's NOT your job to sell them that next project, it's your job to earn their trust by spending time together, showing what you're made of and being, well, trustworthy.

Sometimes it helps to look in the rear view mirror

I'm not usually much of a fan of looking backwards. I tend to be far more interested in what's ahead, what's going to happen tomorrow. You know, 'got that t-shirt' and all.

But once in a while, there are some really important things to be learned by looking in the rear view mirror. For example, sometimes it's difficult to predict whether or not an opportunity for a given project type, project size or a particular client is going to result in a profitable and successful project. But hindsight is usually 20/20 and there's a way to use your past projects to predict what's likely going to happen the next time. The process is called 'Closed Jobs Analysis' and it will give you insight that can be startling.

Here's how it works. Collect the following data on ALL projects going back at least two, or preferably three or four years and place it into a simple spreadsheet: Gross revenue, net revenue, profit, labor hours, project type (your categories), project size (your definitions) client type, project manager. Once you've entered the data, start sorting for profitability as influenced by the various criteria and look for patterns.

And oh the patterns you'll find! I can't predict which variables influence profit, but invariably there is a trigger that has been a consistent indicator of winning or losing projects. Examples from two firms will highlight how this works and the results that can be seen.

Firm One conducted an analysis of all projects completed during the past three years. There were no patterns of profitability based on project type or client type, but when project size was the central variable the firm made a huge discovery. When looking at individual projects, those with total fees below $12,000 accounted for more than 35% of labor costs, but just 17% of profit. When the cutoff was raised to fees of $25,000, these accounted for almost 55% of labor but just 22% of profits.

In other words, if the firm stayed far away from projects with fees below $25,000, they would have cut their labor hours by 90% and still made more than 60% of their profit! Needless to say, following the analysis they were much more careful about taking on those small projects.

Firm Two also conducted an analysis of projects from the past three years. In their case project size had no impact on profitability, but project type was a huge influence. With fees totaling about $2.25 million after about 18,000 labor hours, profits were around 12% at just under $270,000. But of six project type categories, two, accounting for almost $350,000 in revenue and 5,000 hours of labor, did not make a penny in the aggregate. In fact they combined for a net loss of about $55,000.

The analysis showed that the vast majority of the firm's profits came from three of the six project types. If the three poor performers were eliminated completely the company's revenue would have dropped from $2.25 million to $1.3 million, labor hours would have dropped from 18,000 to less than 8,000 and profit would have INCREASED from $270,000 to more than $320,000!

Firm Three found that just a handful of Project Managers were responsible for the vast majority of profit. And another handful were just going along for the ride!

If you're interested in maximizing profitability, Closed Jobs Analysis is an exercise that you simply must do.

They could be giants

Dion Lewis is a running back for the New England Patriots. He's 5'-8" tall and weighs 195 pounds.

Calais Campbell is a defensive end for the Arizona Cardinals. He's 6'-8" tall and weighs 310 pounds.

That makes Calais 17.6% taller and 59% heavier than Dion.

Yet every Sunday, Dion enthusiastically grabs the ball from Tom Brady and heads, full speed, into four guys that look just like Calais, not to mention the seven others who are lined up behind, ready to pound him into the earth. And the idiot's smiling!!

What is he thinking!?

He's thinking the same thing you need to be thinking when you go head-to-head in a presentation against one of those mega-firms that seem to have unlimited resources to draw on when it comes to impressing a client.

I'm sure you've run into them – those teams that show up with a 3D model, fly-through videos and four-part harmony. You're left standing there with your PowerPoint bullets, wondering what happened. How can a small firm, with limited resources, compete against the big boys who can bring it all?

You've heard that rule of the Old West – never bring a knife to a gunfight. So the first step in winning this battle is to avoid the gunfights. Determine for yourself whether or not the client is likely to be dazzled by all the whiz-bang fireworks. If so, walk away. You don't need that kind of client.

Or, are they open to hearing and seeing genuine enthusiasm, real creativity and dedicated hard work. While the big boys might have the horsepower, there's often a lot of bureaucratic inertia behind it.

If you watch Dion, you realize that he never willfully runs head first into a 300-pound defensive lineman. He cuts, dodges, ducks and dives around the big, lumbering opponent, daring to be caught. He relies on quickness, dexterity and speed, rather than sheer volume.

You can do the same.

No, you can't win a head-to-head, impress-me-if-you-can contest. But you can play a totally different game. Look for the weaknesses in your opponent. Can you out-perform them in client service? Response time? How about flexibility and willingness to do things the way the client would prefer?

Where your 6'-5" opponent has lots of muscle, you've got an endless supply of stories in which you've gone the extra mile for your clients. You've got the close personal relationships that have you sharing barbeque with that client as your kids play together in the back yard.

The best game you can bring is one of enthusiasm and authenticity. Let that client know that you're genuinely excited about working on the project. Let them see who you really are – warts and all. Let them see a level of dedication, passion and commitment that they've never seen before. Let it be infectious. Shy and reserved is for losers. Give it all you've got, and leave absolutely nothing in the locker room.

When Dion Lewis crosses the scrimmage line he knows there are 11 enormous guys, all wanting his head. Anybody else would turn tail and run. But Dion knows he's got something they don't. He genuinely believes he's the best man on the field. He genuinely believes that his speed and agility can beat their size and weight every time. And he genuinely believes that the passion he brings to the field is what wins games.

What do you believe?

Read any good books lately?

If you look up the best-selling authors of all time, you'll find names such as Agatha Christie, Danielle Steel, Dr. Seuss, J.K. Rowling, Jackie Collins and Stephen King. Not exactly what you'd call 'high-brow literature,' is it? But this crowd obviously knows a thing or two about writing a popular book and there are some valuable lessons for those of us who have to communicate to our clients.

While you might not be trying to be the next John Grisham, I'll bet you'd like your audience (i.e., your clients) to read, understand and like what you've written. So it's worthwhile to pay attention.

James V. Smith, Jr. is a novelist and a guy who writes books about writing books. In other words, he teaches wannabe authors how to write the next best seller. He's spent a lot of time analyzing best-selling novels and discovered some remarkable statistics about readability.

Of particular note was the number of characters per word. He found that best sellers of any genre all had a letters-per-word count of less than 4.5. Most were less than 4.3 In fact, the lower it was, the better the seller. Said another way, you should use short words.

In your case, 'Use' is always better than 'Utilize.' 'Do,' instead of 'Perform.' 'Start,' rather than 'Inception.' 'Move,' in place of 'Relocate.' As Mark Twain once said, "Why should I write 'metropolis' when I get paid the same for 'city?'"

The most popular authors also use short sentences. Apparently a sentence's reading ease is inversely related to how many words are in it. For example, a one-word sentence would be understood by 99% of people. A 10-word sentence can be understood by 90% and so on. I once came across a single sentence in an engineering proposal that contained 109 words! You do the math.

Too often, we feel the need to use big words and complex sentences because we think it sounds impressive or intelligent. Nope.

It just sounds hard to read.

Your goal should be for your writing to sound like you talk. Imagine meeting someone who said, "It gives us great pleasure to announce that, effective January 1st, we will be initiating operations in our new Atlanta office. Should you require further information please contact our headquarters." I'd hate to have a whole conversation with that guy!

Instead you're much more likely to say, "We're opening a new office in Atlanta next year and hope it makes things more convenient for you. Please call us if you have any questions."

David Ogilvy is considered by many to be the father of modern advertising and was responsible for a revolution in how companies communicate with their customers. Concerning writing, he said, "I don't know the rules of grammar... If you're trying to persuade people to do something, or buy something, it seems to me you should use their language, the language they use every day, the language in which they think. We try to write in the vernacular."

So if you want to make your writing more understandable, easily read and persuasive, do this: Before you write anything, say it. Out loud. Then write down what you said.

Following the rules?

Don't ya just love it when you work hard to play by the rules and then get beat out when the other guy cheats? Makes you wish your mother had brought you up with a little more pirate in your veins!

But when the people who make them, break the very rules they insist you follow, it's easy to really get steamed.

The Brooks Act was put in place to protect Federal agencies from the self-destructive habit of selecting on low price rather than qualifications. Smart move, Congressman Brooks! But budget-strapped agencies regularly do an end run around the rules, thinking they're being frugal, crafty and smart.

I've heard from plenty of firms who've encountered federal agencies that word their RFPs in such a way that they manage to skirt the QBS rules. Of course everyone suffers when this happens. The firms offering quality services aren't awarded the project, the agency wastes its money on shoddy work and the end users of the project get short-changed when it doesn't work as needed.

Now I'm not telling you anything you didn't already know. I suspect what you'd like to know is, what to do when you encounter that agency that's making your life difficult while simultaneously shooting itself in the foot.

I don't think you're going to like the answer.

The problem with inviting a 500-pound gorilla into your living room is that you pretty much have to do what he says. Federal agencies are kinda like that. They (sometimes rightly) figure they're the big noise and, if you want to play in their game, you'll play by their rules.

When you find yourself on the losing end of an unfair fight, you've got a few options:

First, you can lower your own prices and beat them at their own game. If you choose this route don't forget to put an ironclad definition around the scope of work and charge for every nickel, dime and even penny that falls outside it. This is how the contractors make their money. Low bid wins the job. Extras restore the profit.

Second, you can protest. Get your lawyer involved. Call them on their playing fast and loose with Federal procurement laws. And then let me know how that works out for you. After 40 years in this business, I've never seen it end well.

Finally, you can decide you don't like their game, take your ball and go home. No one is holding a gun to your head and forcing you to chase work that is given to the lowest bidder.

Yes, your firm has probably been serving that market for many years. But markets and clients evolve and there reaches a point where you have to decide if it's worthwhile to continue pursuing a lost cause.

That 500-pound gorilla is going to dance to his own music no matter what you do or say. Maybe it's time to think about going to a different concert.

Problems

Our flight was delayed an hour the other night and we had to run like maniacs through the Minneapolis airport to make the connection.

- I ran into some significant technical glitches while delivering an online program last week and had to endure high blood pressure, severe annoyance and likely additional hair loss.
- I found a scratch on the rear door of my car today where some thoughtless idiot dragged his belt buckle past it in the grocery store parking lot.

Oh, I could go on.

But when I catch myself wallowing in the problems that plague my life, I like to stop, do a little mental pivot, and see this disaster from a different perspective.

- We made the flight and, somehow, the miracle-working baggage handlers got our suitcases onto the next flight in four minutes flat! The aircraft mechanics had ensured the plane was flight-ready, the ramp crew loaded it with fuel, the pilots got us safely home and the flight attendant asked if I'd prefer red or white. Thanks, Delta!
- The tech support team helped us work out the glitch, our students were as kind and understanding as could be and people on my team stepped up to carry the ball when I was the victim of a windstorm that took out my internet connection in Vancouver. Thanks, folks!
- I have a comfortable, reliable (and even slightly indulgent) car that I can drive anywhere I want in comfort and style. I have a grocery store that is conveniently located, stocks far more than I could ever possibly eat and is staffed with the most friendly, helpful people you'll ever meet. Thanks Jaguar and Publix!

I've got problems all right.

I also have blessings. More than I could ever begin to count. And the blessings I enjoy so staggeringly overwhelm whatever I might label as a problem, that I'm ashamed when I catch myself complaining about anything.

To even describe them as 'First World' problems would give my so-called trials more weight and importance and give myself more self-indulgence than either of us deserve.

I think about Paris. I think about Syria. I think about children around the world who are hungry, thirsty, lonely and scared.

I have no problems. Only gratitude. And obligations.

How much should you spend on marketing?

One of the most common ways of setting an annual marketing budget is also one of the dumbest – look to see what the other guy is spending. It's dumb for two reasons. First, who's to say the other guy is spending wisely?

Second, determining reliable statistics in this industry is virtually impossible. The design professions are a relatively small industry in comparison to the world of business in general. So there aren't that many people trying to track the numbers. And those who try, bump into very small sample sizes and inconsistent reporting.

Nonetheless, between the available statistics and the anecdotal evidence, it's possible to reach some conclusions. Keep in mind that these numbers are conjured from a combination of industry statistics, anecdotal evidence and a bit of guesswork. But that's the best we've got.

Fewer than half of all firms prepare a marketing budget. Those that do plan to spend about 3.5% of net revenue on all marketing activities. (Net revenue is your total revenue, minus pass-through fees to other consultants and reimbursable expenses). Those that track their spending find that they spend a little more than 5% of net revenue.

Without getting down in the weeds of upper and lower quartiles and median versus mean, here's how that spending tends to break down.

Marketing Staff Labor	35%
Other Marketing Labor	15% - 20%
Proposals	5% - 15%
Client Entertainment	4% - 6%
Travel	2% - 6%
Brand Building Activities	7% - 14%

Is this spending wise? I tend not to think so. Most of these numbers come from the rear view mirror with little or no thought put into what ought to be spent and what it ought to be spent on.

To put this into perspective, the average small business spends 9-12% of revenue on marketing. In other words, architecture and engineering firms spend less than half that.

How do you make your spending smarter? First, don't try to make a budget yet. Begin by simply tracking your spending – accurately and honestly. It's going to take at least two years of tracking your expenditures before you're able to develop a marketing budget that has any useful accuracy.

Think about what you want your marketing investments to do for you – build your brand, build client loyalty, get selected for projects.Then examine your expenditures in each area and do some rudimentary ROI calculations. You want to work towards being able to set goals for both spending and ROI in the future. As you begin to allocate spending, plan to put about 80% of your budget towards retaining and growing your existing clients. Spend 20% to find new ones.

Don't believe anyone who says you should be spending some set percentage of revenue. They're wrong. You should spend what it takes to accomplish your marketing goals. If you want to grow, expand into a new region or market sector, increase your marketing spending temporarily. If you're driving a car at 30 mph and want to accelerate to 60, you have to step on the gas. Once you're up to the higher speed, you can back off on the accelerator and 'cruise' along the highway. So increase your marketing budget in growth years. Decrease it in times of 'status quo'.

The Achilles Heel in content marketing

It's Monday evening about seven. Twelve hours from now, the first of more than 15,000 people will open their email and find a subject line saying, **"The Achilles Heel in Content Marketing"** smiling from their Inbox. Better than 10% will open it, and a smaller number will click on a link that's embedded.

The ONLY reason you read it, the ONLY right I have to be in your inbox and take precious moments from your day is that, in return, I give you something valuable. Something you'll find useful today or down the road.

The technique is called **Content Marketing**. If you've got something to sell, you first have to establish credibility with your potential customers. You do this by giving away (with no strings attached) 'free samples' of information that are useful and valuable to potential customers.

If your stuff is good enough, if it's widely read and shared around, you begin to establish yourself as a thought leader. Keep it up long enough, with information that's high quality enough, and you begin to collect a loyal following. Supplement this ripple effect long enough with social media and eventually somebody's going to conclude that you might be worth talking to.

Simple, huh!?

But did you notice the, "if your stuff is good enough…" and the, "if you keep it up long enough…" bits? Those are the tricky parts. I see way too many 'blogs' that are an endless collection of links to some other body's ideas. They're lame. They're time wasters. They're quickly unsubscribed.

If you're going to go down the Content Marketing road, there are three things you have to get right.

First, you have to have content that clients and prospective clients want to read. They DO NOT want to read about you. The fact that you won an award ranks 197th on their list of Most-

Important-Things in a day. They have zero interest in the project you've just been awarded. And while the fact that you've recently hired a new Project Manager might be meaningful to his mother, the rest of the world isn't listening.

Second, you have to convey this great content through writing that's worth reading. It has to be engaging, entertaining and ever-so-worthwhile. The simple recitation of facts puts us to sleep and boring us is a sure-fire link to the unsubscribe button. No, the writing has to be good. And that means it's been created by A Writer. Someone with training, skill and experience in stringing words together that people actually want to read. If that's not you, find a professional writer who can translate your thoughts into captivating, page-turning prose.

Finally, you have to do it over, and over and over again. You accomplish nothing if you write a blog once. Or if you do it occasionally, sporadically or intermittently. This blog has been running every week, without fail, for years. Most of the time, I've got tons of topic ideas and way too much to say. But I'll admit that there are some Monday evenings when I'm sitting at this keyboard and I've got nothing! But I know that if I miss an entry I'll go all the way back to the start without collecting $200.

Content Marketing is a fabulous way to build your brand if…

Oops, sorry, I've got to go. They tell me there's a blog post due.

So what?

The firm had asked me to conduct a training seminar on presentation skills and we'd spent the better part of the day with the video camera recording people laboring through the slides, boards and scripts of their most recent interviews. Without fail, each time someone got up to speak, they turned their back on the audience and watched as slide after slide of past projects shot onto the screen.

I patiently reminded them that they needed to let the audience know WHY they should be looking at a particular slide and what benefit they could expect to gain from that knowledge. But, as the afternoon wore on, it was obvious that I wasn't getting through.

In desperation I pulled out a big fat marker and wrote "So What?" on a piece of paper. Every time someone would say, "And here's another project we've done..." I would hold up the sign and force them to explain the relevance. It was a painful process and I wasn't sure the lesson was really sinking in. So I decided to raise the stakes.

The company had an interview coming up the following week and I made them a dare. I dared them to invite the selection committee to use the "So What?" signs.

They were in the mood for risk taking so we used the laser printer to prepare some professional-looking signs and mounted them on popsicle-stick handles. (How professional can a sign that says, "So What?" be?)

As the presentation team introduced themselves at the interview they handed one sign to each member of the review panel. They instructed the panel that, if at any time during the interview they felt their time was being wasted or the team was talking about things that didn't seem relevant, they were to hold up their signs.

They thought this a bit odd, but the novelty was intruiging and they'd sat through too many lifeless interviews to object.

It wasn't long before the old habits started to surface. One of the presenters slipped comfortably into his old routine of showing off his slide collection with his back to the audience. But this time, someone held up their "So What?" sign.

The presenter stopped, thanked the client for helping him improve the quality of his presentation, and pointed out that the construction techniques used in the project shown were going to be used to solve a very similar problem on the current project.

From that point on the interview was completely changed. Every time someone held up a "So What?" sign (which quickly become a fun game for the client), not only did everyone have a good laugh, the stuffy monologue was converted to a high energy dialogue. There was an electric exchange of ideas and the interview was actually fun for them all.

When they'd finished, the client handed them the project on the spot. In their words, "Anyone who has the nerve to come in here with signs like this is the kind of company we want to work with." But they had one condition: they insisted on keeping the "So What?" signs because, "We attend plenty of meetings where these would be really handy!"

Here's something you already knew

Expensive wine tastes better.

Hold on!, you say. That's not true! How often have you prided yourself on buying a $7 bottle of Blackbeard's Revenge and commenting on how it's just as good as the $45 bottle of Chateau le Peuff that you had last week?

Turns out the same neuro transmitters are responsible for both results.

A study by researchers from Cal Tech and Stanford found that the intensity of pleasure we experience from a glass of wine is directly connected to its price. The study, tongue-twistingly titled, "Marketing actions can modulate neural representations of experienced pleasantness" used functional magnetic resonance imaging (FMRI) to monitor the medial orbitofrontal cortex – the pleasure center of the brain – of wine connoisseurs who tasted wines after hearing stories about them.

The result? Even though they were drinking the identical Cabernet Sauvignon, when they were told that one glass had a dramatically higher price than another, they invariably found it to be better.

Several other studies have also found related conclusions. For example, knowing the ingredients and brand of a beer can affect the reported taste quality. Expectations about a new film can affect how much you enjoy it (can you say, *Star Wars*?). And the most interesting study found that the price of an energy drink can influence your ability to solve puzzles!

What's the takeaway for your firm? There is much more to persuading a client to select you and pay the premium fee you're asking than simply communicating your capabilities. One of the important conclusions of the Cal Tech/Stanford study was that, "Contrary to the basic assumptions of economics, marketing can successfully affect experienced pleasantness by manipulating nonintrinsic attributes of goods."

In other words, they're not buying based on the merits of the services you offer. Just as with beer, wine and cars, there is a whole host of intangible factors that influence your client's decision. And the more you are aware of and make use of those intangibles in your marketing communications, the more successful your selling efforts will be.

So don't just list your services. Tell great stories about your firm. Don't simply list the projects you've completed, build an aura of accomplishment and success around them. Don't simply talk about designing or constructing roads, buildings and bridges, tell us how you're making the world a better place!

As for why you believe the $7 bottle tastes better than the best the French have to offer, if you've convinced yourself that you're a bargain magnet, your taste buds are going to back you all the way.

How do you feel?

Well there we have it. Another anniversary, another 365 under your belt and a mixed bag to show for it.

I'm sure that as you look back you're noting some accomplishments of which you're justifiably proud. Go ahead, pat yourself on the back and strut a little!

But I bet you can also see those moments and missteps that you'd just as soon forget. Those inglorious choices that remind us all just how human, imperfect and frequently just plain dumb we all can be.

So as you close the books on this one and get ready to crank up for 365 more, how do you feel?

Do you feel revved up, with that 'Let-me-in-Coach!' fire in your belly? Or are you just tired, with a one-foot-in-front-of-the-other resignation that comes at the end of an arduous, uphill climb? Are you champing at the bit to be let loose into this opportunity-filled New Year? Or are you looking for a place to pull off and rest?

I find that my reality tends to reflect my thoughts. Which is very different than having my thoughts reflect my reality. If my thoughts are tending towards judgment and blame, I find that my days fill up with inconvenient circumstances, annoying people and disagreeable tasks to be done.

But if I deliberately choose to entertain thoughts of excitement, anticipation and delight, my days are invariably a succession of curious and memorable events, unique and interesting people and challenging, yet rewarding tasks to be done.

So I resolve to feel good this next year. All the time! I will meet no dull people. I will take on no boring task. I will find no one to blame for whatever might happen to me. Because, as I look either back over the past year or ahead to the next, I discover that I was the only one who was consistently present for it all. Whatever befell me, it's highly likely that I was largely responsible. Whatever is to come, I am, for the most part, in control.

I can't make myself taller, or younger, or smarter or better looking. But I can make myself happier, more curious, more enthusiastic, more optimistic, more excited. And so, that's how I choose to feel. How do YOU feel?

Selling hours by the pound

What is the highest hourly rate that anyone in your firm has ever charged to any client to do anything?

Yeah, you understood that right. The highest, most audacious, almost embarrassing billing rate ever. Was it $300? $425? Ever hit $500? Near as I can tell, most firms cap out at somewhere south of $400 an hour. And that's for the really high value stuff like expert witness work.

And what does this mean? Taken at face value, it means that no one is capable, in the span of one hour, of doing anything worth more than 400 bucks.

Does this seem as nutty to you as it does to me?

When was the last time you attended a permitting or zoning meeting on behalf of a client and negotiated a concession that saved them thousands? When was the last time you were suddenly hit with a brilliant solution to a complex problem that had been costing your client tens, or even hundreds, of thousands of dollars?

And what did you bill for that one-hour meeting? What did you charge for that lighting-bolt idea? Tell me your billing rate again…

Your clients don't want an hour of your time. They want the project successfully completed.

Granted, there are some things that are best paid for by the hour. Massage for example – the longer it goes on, the better you feel. But if you paid your dentist by the hour, a routine cleaning might go on all day! Imagine paying a heart surgeon by the hour. You don't want the surgery to last a long time. You just want it to be successful.

Want to hear something ridiculous? I ran into a firm once that had a published rate schedule that included 17 different rate categories. Engineer 1, 2, 3…, CAD technician 1,2,3…, it went on and on. But here's the great thing – there were just 11 people in the firm! Who needs this kind of ludicrousness?

I want you to resolve that you'll do everything in your power to avoid hourly rates. Don't talk to your clients about how many hours you'll spend, talk about the value you'll bring. Don't talk about multipliers, talk about one lump-sum, all-inclusive price that includes everything.

You didn't go to school to learn how to count hours and keep timesheets. You became an expert in your field so you could solve big problems and make the world a better place. Let's resolve to think like professional problem solvers.

The secret to a great client debrief

You've poured your heart (not to mention more than a few long nights) into the proposal only to be told you came second. At that point it's easy to walk away and leave the experience behind you. Not only is it painful to dwell on the loss, there's another urgent proposal waiting to be written.

But to walk away without touching base with the client is to leave behind a golden opportunity to build a stronger relationship, increase the quality of future proposals and drive up the odds of winning in the next round.

Even when firms do conduct debriefs, they tend to be ineffective because of the way questions are asked. The commonly asked questions – some variation on 'Please tell us how we did' – result in noncommittal answers – some variation on 'Yours was one of many good proposals; It was a tough decision; Please continue to submit on future RFPs; etc.' These give you no real feedback and provide no real guidance for your next proposal.

The secret to a good debrief is to give your client *permission* to constructively criticize. Instead of vague, open-ended questions such as 'How did we do?' ask specific questions that invite real feedback about your proposal:

- Please tell me the three things you liked most about our proposal.
- Please tell me the three things you liked least about it.
- What would you like to see changed in the next proposal we submit that might increase our chances of winning?
- What did the winning firm include in their proposal that put them over the top?
- When you think about the proposals that have won your projects in recent years, what are the common traits that made them stand out from the rest?

Questions worded in this way make it clear that you are seeking specific advice and that you won't be offended by the answers. They politely invite and give permission for criticism.

I n addition to increasing the quality of future proposals, there are other real advantages to proposal debriefs conducted this way.

- The client sees that you are truly interested in improving your submittals
- You demonstrate your long-term interest in them
- You have an opportunity to further enhance your relationship and increase the odds of winning the next project.

Never pass on the opportunity to conduct a debrief after you've submitted a losing proposal. And while you're at it, why not conduct the same debrief even when you've won?

9.63 seconds

At the Summer Olympics in 2012 the gold medal in the 100-meter dash went to Usain Bolt of Jamaica. He finished in an incredible 9.63 seconds. What I find amazing is not so much that there is an individual who possess such skill, talent and strength, but that there are so many of them.

While Mr. Bolt won the gold, the next five runners all crossed the finish line no more than 35/100th of a second later. Since it takes between 300 and 400 milliseconds to close and reopen your eyelid, all six men crossed the line in the proverbial blink of an eye.

Every runner in that race beat out thousands of others just to earn a starting spot in that race. Every runner was a champion many times over with world-class performances in the years leading up to and following the Olympics.

Now think about that project you're trying to win. And think about the competitors who want to win it away from you. The unqualified and the mediocre were weeded out long ago and those who are left in the race have demonstrated stellar performance many times over. Those competitors have a bulls eye taped to your back and won't rest until they win the gold.

Since it was first set at 12 seconds in the first Olympics of the modern era, the winning time for the 100 meters has steadily fallen. And no one expects that trend to change. Just as no one expects your competitors to ease up, back off or otherwise cut you the least bit of slack. They're determined to win those clients from you and won't rest until they do.

To stay in front you must be constantly raising the bar on your performance. But so often I see firms taking the easy road when it comes to writing top-notch proposals and delivering gold medal presentations. They're phoning in a 'good-enough' performance and using that old fallback, the 'Save As' technique, to crank out yet another middling proposal.

It's hard to stay at the top of your game. Damn hard. But while silver and bronze medals are offered to the almost-as-goods in the Olympics, second, third and last in the races you run give you squat. In our game it's gold or go home.

The other day I was chatting with a Principal at a firm who told me about a client they've had for the last nine years. In the most recent re-up on their long-term contract, the client assured them that they didn't have to work too hard as the project had their name on it.

It's way too easy to sit back and relax when the job is yours to loose. Fortunately this firm understands the danger of taking things for granted and used the opportunity to raise the bar even further with their proposal submission. Their client was blown away with the firm's fresh new ideas and never-rest-on-your-laurels attitude. Their competitors were reminded that a gold medal champion is a force to be reckoned with.

At the next Summer Olympicx, eight men will settle into the starting blocks and then give their all for the next 10 seconds. Only one, however, will come away with gold. What are you willing to invest in your next race?

How to steal from your competitors

Samsung loves Apple. Toyota loves Honda. Marriott loves Hyatt. And you should love your competitors too.

Competitors keep us on our toes. They prevent us from becoming complacent and taking our clients for granted. And they force us to grow. So, given that your competitors are offering you all these benefits, I believe that you should take everything you can from them.

It's really easy to talk trash about competitors. They're not playing at your level. They don't treat their clients as well as you do. Their offices aren't nearly as much fun to work in as yours. But the fact is, they're actually pretty good at what they do. That you call them competitors means that, on any given day, they could win out over you. There have to be at least some clients who think they're better than you, or they would've chosen you instead of them.

Let's assume, that maybe, just maybe, they know some things you don't, can do some things you can't and are, in some ways, superior to you. What a great opportunity for you to steal from them! Before you go thinking that I'm advocating larceny or employee poaching, let me explain. The best thing to steal from your competitors is their wisdom.

What are the five best things they did last year? What did they do that surprised you and showed you a new way of thinking? What did they decide that would have been counter to your instincts, but ended up working? Who did they hire that you passed up? And what did they do that you hadn't though of to turn that employee into a profitable asset?

In many ways, your competitors are smarter than you. And the perspective that you have, being outside the close quarters of their firm, lets you see that wisdom in action in a way that they, themselves, might not even be able to perceive.

While you're admiring and learning from the brilliant moves

they've made, analyze the mistakes they've made too. Not from a perspective of criticism or scorn, but from the valuable lessons you can learn by observing their experience.

Think of your competitors as the source of a ringside seat to a free collection of Harvard Business Journal case studies. If you only pay attention, you'll realize that there are invaluable lessons to be learned in a safe, risk-free environment.

Your competitors can be a pain in the butt. But they can also be a source of tremendous knowledge. It's okay to steal from them, as long as it's just the wisdom they have to offer.

Have you forgotten already?

Hen you stand up to make a presentation, I'm guessing that you'd like the audience to remember what you've said for more than a few fleeting seconds. Unfortunately, recall following the average business presentations is shorter than a Kardashian marriage.

Dr. Carmen Simon is a cognitive scientist who's done extensive research on presentations and memory. Her Twitter handle, @areyoumemorable, says it all. A few years ago she conducted a research project to determine how many slides people actually remember from a typical PowerPoint presentation

More than 1,500 participants were invited to view a short, online PowerPoint presentation of 20 slides. Participants were randomly assigned to view different versions of the presentation. After 48 hours, they were asked to recall anything they could remember about the presentation. She reached some important conclusions that you'd do well to consider when you're getting ready for your next presentation:

- People can only hold about four or five items at a time in short term memory. The important thing is therefore to make sure that we point them at the right things to remember. In other words, just because it's on the slide, don't expect them to remember it. You have to reinforce what they're seeing.
- People remember the unusual. If everything in a presentation is equally intense or equally bland you have no control over what, if anything, people will remember. That means, if all your slides are on the same corporate template, we won't remember anything.
- Concrete visual language aids recall. In layperson terms that means you need to make maximum use of graphics, images and pictures, and leave the text on your slides to a minimum.

- It helps to group your slides and 'chunk' your presentation into sections. This can be done by the color of the text or the background, or by the use of a different set of images. Well thought out connections between different parts of a presentation are more important than just pushing more content.
- People crave novelty. They are more likely to remember what they find new and surprising, rather than what they find familiar. Where information differs from what we would expect, we sit up and take notice.
- Repetition and alliteration helps. Using the same word, or finding three or four words that begin with the same letter to stress your key points will probably make the ideas stick in the mind.

It's way too easy to kid yourself that, because you had the information on a slide, your audience is going to remember it. But communication is far more of a subtle art than that. Next time you're getting ready for a presentation, identify the (very few) key points you want to make, then plan how you're going to repeat, reinforce, visualize, highlight and bang a drum in the hope that recall can be extended just a little bit longer.

On average, marketing spending averages are stupid

Fact #1: On average, design firms spend about five percent of their net revenues on marketing.

Fact #2: This questionable piece of information is less than useless.

Yet I'm asked about this so-called statistic all the time. As if the average of a group of rolled-up numbers that aren't consistently measured and have been collected from a sampling that is too small to be statistically relevant, is somehow going to be of use to you.

The average American male has a size 9 foot. But if you're ordering a pair for yourself you'd do well to measure your own feet. Same rule applies when you're thinking about your marketing spending. So instead of asking about industry averages and then cramming your foot into a shoe that's too small (or floating around in one that's too big) you should ask what you're trying to accomplish with your marketing spending and what that might cost.

Near as we can tell, less than half of firms actually prepare a marketing budget. If your firm is one of those that doesn't, it's time to start working on that. But don't fire up the spreadsheet just yet. It's going to take you at least two years of tracking your expenditures before you're able to develop a marketing budget that has any useful accuracy.

So don't try to develop a budget yet. Just keep careful track of what you are spending, do some rudimentary ROI calculations and work towards being able to set goals for both spending and ROI in the future.

As much as we crave those averages as we attempt to find some rationale for our own actions, they don't help in real-world decision-making. For example, let's say your firm wants to grow by expanding into a new region or market sector. That doesn't happen by itself so you're going to have to, at least temporarily, increase your marketing investment.

If you're driving a car at 30 mph and you want to accelerate to 60, you have to burn some gas. Once you're up to the higher speed, you can back off on the accelerator and 'cruise' along the highway.

If your firm is in a highly competitive, crowded market, you're going to have to make more noise than the next guy in order to stand out from the crowd. Playing the averages leads you to be, well, average. Another word for which might be 'commodity.'

Averages always hide the valuable information. Where are the extremes, the outliers? What do the firms who spend just two percent get for their investment? Why are some firms choosing to spend 10 or 12 percent, and what do they have to show for it?

"Average revenues in our branch offices were up 12% last year." Turns out that two offices doubled their sales while the rest were stagnant or even shrunk. Wouldn't you find the detail to be more important and useful than the average?

The curse of competence

Your firm does really good work. Your buildings don't fall down. Your treatment plants perform to spec. Your control systems operate flawlessly.

Well done, You!

But there's a problem.

Your competitors do really good work too. Competence is everywhere. It's assumed. And it's no longer valued.

Pull out a recent proposal that you've submitted to any client and read through it. You'll discover that you're selling competence. Here's a real example with the names changed:

Acme Engineering has extensive experience with conducting and reviewing HUD Environmental Assessments in accordance with the National Environmental Policy Act (NEPA) and 24 CFR Part 58. In addition to conducting the Environmental Assessments for 26 projects in Jefferson County worth approximately $210 million, Acme provided quality control reviews for the remaining 41 regional projects in surrounding counties.

Man, are these folks capable! But so are dozens, if not hundreds of other firms. Mere competence isn't what's needed anymore.

What's needed in today's cash-strapped, deficit-ridden, multi-priority and overwhelmingly complicated world is innovative, creative solutions to a whole new class of really sticky problems. How can we replace a crumbling infrastructure when we're up to our ears in debt? Tackle THAT problem and you'll be in demand everywhere.

While it may sound glib, you're doing the easy stuff. You're solving the easy problems. The same problems that thousands of firms can solve.

Are you making a contribution to this new class of really tough tests or are you waiting for someone else to solve them so you can do the easy stuff? Your firm's future depends on these big challenges being solved. So what unexpected team are you assembling? What non-traditional but vital talents are you adding? What strange bedfellows are you joint venturing with in order to tackle these unprecedented challenges?

If we wait around for someone else to define the problem, create the scope of work and figure out how to pay for it, there'll be no shortage of talent who are then ready to find a 'solution.' But today's challenges and your firm's oh-so-profitable future lie in those difficult first three steps. What is your firm doing to play on THAT stage? Someone has to solve these problems. Why not you?

When was the last time you sat down with an economist or an investment banker to see how you might pool talents and resources? When was the last time you included a politician on your team so you could redefine the problem and develop a totally unexpected solution? When was the last time you invited someone whose knowledge area was radically different than yours to bring a new perspective to your firm? When was the last time you stuck your toe into some truly different water?

It's time to stop expecting prosperity in exchange for mere competence. It's time to change, to stretch, to go far beyond simple competence and start tackling the really hard problems of today.

You and your team are way beyond competent – you're creative, resourceful and innovative. Can you also be daring?

Keep a 'dossier' on your competitors

James Bond does it. Every large corporation does it. You, too, need to keep a close eye on your competition.

Every time Chrysler comes out with a new mini-van, the first two off the line are purchased by Ford and GM. Every time Apple updates the iPhone, the first ones available are grabbed up by Samsung and LG. They dismantle them, reverse-engineer the systems and features and conduct in-depth analyses of the pricing strategy. Why? Because they can't survive without knowing the activities and strategies of their competitors.

Neither can you.

It's a good idea to maintain a file (let's call it a "dossier," it's so much more like James Bond!) on your main competitors. It could include a printout of their web site, a copy of their brochure, a list of principals and key employees with outline resumes and any other pertinent information about key clients, project histories and known strengths and weaknesses.

Gathering this information isn't hard. Between the Internet, your clients, contractors and sub-consultants and even former employees who might now be working for you, there is lots of information available. Start asking and digging and you'll be amazed at what you can find!

What should you do with the information you gather?

In the long term you need to maintain strong differentiation in the market. If other firms are looking more and more like you everyday, it may be complimentary but it's bad for business. Many of your strategic planning decisions will be based on opportunities and threats that exist in the marketplace. A competitor that is coming on strong is a decided threat.

In the short term this information can help you get more closely 'wired' to your clients. Let's say you're going up against a certain competitor on a new water treatment plant project for a local municipality. Your research tells you that one of your main competitors has recently given a seminar at the regional APWA (American Public Works Association) conference and was very well received. This could give them a strong advantage since the local Public Works Director would be impressed with their obvious expertise. With this knowledge you could:

- Mount an extra effort to build on your personal relationship with the Public Works Director.
- Conduct a short, direct mail program in which you send a series of tips on state-of-the-art treatment plant maintenance and technology to the ten Public Works Directors within a 50-mile radius.
- Investigate pursuing the project as a joint venture with the competitor.
- Connect with a nationally-known consultant who has presented an even more impressive seminar.

There may be other strategies you can implement but the point is, each of these strategies acknowledges the reality of the marketplace. Without this information you would walk in blind and then wonder why the other guys ate your lunch.

Making out like a bandit

I work with a lot of business developers. The vast majority of them fall into that broad category that we call the 'Seller-Doer.' Otherwise known as the 'Eat-What-You-Kill' model of business development.

Most of these great folks got into the business because they like the 'Doer' side of that title. But somewhere along the road, they hoisted the 'Seller' responsibility onto their backs and discovered that the load can be a lot heavier.

Much of the reluctance that I hear comes in the form of, "I don't want to appear pushy." "I don't like coming across as a 'hard seller." "I don't want to come across as a used car salesman."

I understand those sentiments. They're rooted in the perception that you're trying to convince someone to buy something they neither want nor need. I, too, will never push something on someone who really doesn't need or want it. But I invite you to adopt a different point of view. One that just might revolutionize your attitude towards business development.

I invite you to think back to a project you did a couple of years ago. Make sure you pick one that was really successful, the client loved it and everybody walked away a winner. And make sure it was at least two years back. Got it?

OK, now think about the fee you were paid. I hope it was a fair fee and that you felt good about the compensation you received for the work you did.

But have you spent it yet? Do you still have any of that money hanging around? Are you still deriving benefit from the fee that client paid? Or, do you have to now find other projects in order to keep the cash flowing? My guess is that the money's long gone. It was nice while it lasted, but let's face it, that was two years ago...

Now, I want you to think about your client. Are they still enjoying the results of the work you did? Is the project still providing returns, benefits and positive cash flow for them? If you designed a bridge, I'm sure they're still driving over it. The treatment plant is still working as planned. The new library is still being referred to as, 'the NEW library,' and the housing development is still providing returns to the developer.

I'm sure all those clients have long since stopped thinking about the fee they paid (regardless of the griping they did at the time!) but they're surely still glowing about how smart they were to do the project and to hire you to do it!

So who came out as the biggest winner? Who did the biggest favor for whom?

The fact is that your clients ALWAYS come out ahead when they hire you. And that reluctance you have about selling? Kinda misdirected, isn't it?!

The fact is that selling your services isn't something you do TO that client. It's something you do FOR them.

So let's stop apologizing for selling your services and realize just how invaluable you are.

Sharpies and post-it notes

S ave As...
      That's where most presentations begin. Take something we've done before, rework it, reuse as much of it as possible, change a few names and references and it's good to go. That might work for you, but it's a complete rip-off for those you're presenting to. They expect and deserve a lot more.

So how should you begin to begin to get ready for your presentation?

First, and most important of all, DON'T start by opening PowerPoint. In fact, stay as far away from a computer keyboard as you can.

Instead, start with a pad of Post-It notes (the 4-inch kind,) a felt-tip Sharpie and a blank wall. That's all you need to start planning the best presentation you've ever delivered.

Now ask yourself this question: "If, at the end of this presentation, I can expect my audience to remember one and only one thing, what would I like that one thing to be?" When you have your answer, write it on a Post-It and stick in on the wall. Then carry on by asking yourself more questions.

- What are the things I'll have to talk about in order to make that one point?
- What are the secondary points I'll need to make in order to reinforce that point?
- What evidence can I offer that will prove my point?
- What diagrams, photos or graphics could I use to illustrate my point?
- What stories could I tell that support my point?

Think also about how different people might connect with your ideas. How would you explain your point to that classic 'Analytical' personality type? What's the best way to ensure the 'Extrovert' understands it? What about Bob, the Public Works Director – what aspects of your idea is he going to embrace? Resist? And what points will you have to make for him to buy into what you're proposing?

Each time you think of a supporting point, a story, some evidence, a great picture or illustration, write it or sketch it on a Post-It and stick it on the wall. Brainstorm freely without censoring or editing your ideas. Let your thoughts flow and capture each of them – one Post-It per idea – on the wall.

When you've run out of points and new ideas, step back and squint at your wall. Which ideas belong together? Which ones reinforce the others? Move the Post-Its around. Stack them, lump them together, rearrange them as you see connections emerging or ideas forming. Watch as a logical storyboard begins to emerge.

Then walk away from your wall. Come back in an hour and see what's missing. See, also, if anything is extraneous and should be left out. Ask someone else to look at your wall, walk them through it and let them poke holes in your logic, your sequence, your story and your conclusions.

When you've shuffled, mixed, arranged and rearranged your Post-Its enough that they hang together and represent a cohesive idea, you'll see the skeleton of a cohesive story and a compelling presentation right there on the wall.

Then, and only then should you launch your favorite presentation software.

PowerPoint forces you to think linearly. It doesn't let you to visualize your thoughts and then play with them creatively. Brainstorming with a Sharpie and a pad of Post-Its frees your mind to use fluid and lateral thinking and create a far more focuses, compelling, interesting and persuasive presentation.

We will exceed your expectations!

If I had a nickel for every time I've heard someone tell a prospective client that "we will exceed your expectations" I'd be lying on a beach in Margaritaville.

It's a way too common phrase and, on the surface, it makes sense. "Not only will we do what you expect, we'll go above and beyond and startle you with the quality of our work and service."

Nice sentiment, but there are two fatal flaws in the idea. First, how can you exceed my expectations if you don't go to the trouble of finding out what they are? And, while we're at it, exactly when and how do you determine that you've exceeded them and by how much? Because clients hear the phrase so often, and since no one ever inquires or follows up, they've come to see it for the trite drivel it is.

Second, there's a built-in problem when you exceed expectations.

Imagine that you head across the street to McDonald's for lunch today, with the idea of a Big Mac in your immediate future. You've got some expectations about how you'll be greeted, how long it will take and what the burger will look and taste like.

Only this time, the fella behind the counter is polite, sophisticated, intelligent and erudite. Your lunch arrives lickity-split, the fries are fresh and crispy, the lettuce is fresh and the burger actually looks like the ones you see in the ads! Not only that, it's the most delicious burger you've ever tasted!

Your jaw is on the floor and you decide you'll be back tomorrow. Next day, same thing. The people are polite and attentive and the food is better than your Mom's on her best day. Two or three days of this and you've become a Big Mac convert.

Then, four or five days into your McBinge-ing, things go back to normal. The service is merely adequate, the food is ok and the little ketchup thingy squirts onto your shirt. And you? Now you're disappointed.

We have to be careful about exceeding expectations. Because as soon as you do, those expectations go up. Exceed them a few times and those expectations are reset to a new, higher bar. They become the new normal. Dare to fall short of that new standard and we start to wonder if we should take our business elsewhere.

It's very trendy to exhort everyone to exceed expectations. A quick Google search on the phrase got me 177,000,000 results, every one of which is enthusiastically supportive of the idea. But some caution is due: that simple and seductive phrase is too easy to say and way too hard to act on.

Before we go making such trite and un-thought-out statements like, "we will exceed your expectations," how 'bout we start by simply setting them high and working to meet them?

As George Weasley said about the marks he received from Harry Potter's Hogwarts School: "I've always thought Fred and I should've got 'Exceeds Expectations' in everything, because we exceeded expectations just by turning up for the exams."

Are you woolly-minded?

We all write. Emails, letters, proposals, reports and texts pour out of our fingertips, keyboards and pen nibs at a prodigious rate.

Writing is a form of communication, which assumes that we want the reader to understand and then be persuaded, motivated, educated, informed or otherwise moved by the ideas we share. But how effective are we at it?

One of my heroes is David Ogilvy, an advertising genius in the 1950's and '60's and widely considered the father of modern advertising. He was a pioneer of information-rich, soft-sell ads that didn't insult people's intelligence. As an advertising executive and copywriter he knew how to communicate a clear idea and persuade customers to buy.

He was the founder of Ogilvy and Mather, to this day one of the largest advertising agencies in the world. In 1982, he wrote a memo to his employees, titled *"How to Write."* Thirty-five years on, we can still learn from his wisdom.

The better you write, the higher you go in Ogilvy & Mather. People who think well, write well. Woolly-minded people write woolly memos, woolly letters and woolly speeches. Good writing is not a natural gift. You have to learn to write well. Here are 10 hints:

1. **Read the Roman-Raphaelson book on writing. Read it three times.** [You can still buy it on Amazon].
2. **Write the way you talk. Naturally.**
3. **Use short words, short sentences and short paragraphs.**
4. **Never use jargon words like 'reconceptualize,' 'demassification,' 'attitudinally,' 'judgmentally.' They are hallmarks of pretense.**

5. Never write more than two pages on any subject.
6. Check your quotations.
7. Never send a letter or a memo on the day you write it. Read it aloud the next morning—and then edit it.
8. If it is something important, get a colleague to improve it.
9. Before you send your letter or your memo, make sure it is crystal-clear what you want the recipient to do.
10. If you want ACTION, don't write. Go and tell the guy what you want.

A great deal of the writing we do as marketers is intended to persuade our clients to select us, instead of the other guy. But far too much of our writing is dull, flat and uninspiring. As Ogilvy once famously said, "You can't bore your customers into buying your products." When it comes to persuading, motivating, educating, informing or otherwise moving our clients to hire us, it would serve us all well to pay attention.

Six reasons your salespeople are not closing sales

'Sell' is considered a four-letter word within many_firms. But nothing happens till somebody sells something. And if your business developers aren't closing deals on a regular basis, then a whole lotta nuthin' is happening.

One of our clients has a great way of putting it. He calls those business developers who can't or won't close sales, "Professional Visitors." Lots of time spent with clients. Not much to show for it.

If your team isn't closing enough sales, it may be because one or more of these reasons is sabotaging their success.

1. Their leads haven't been pre-qualified
Chasing a prospect that is a bad fit for your services or your firm is simply a waste of time and money. Develop a profile of your ideal client and make sure any new prospect matches it. Does this prospect have the money to pay? Are they used to buying professional services? Are they price shopping? Do your homework before investing in a sales effort.

2. They're not asking the right questions
Many salespeople spend too much time talking about their firm and their services. But the best ones know how to ask the right questions to uncover the prospects' needs and desires. Knowing both what they need and what they want, it becomes easy to align your services with their circumstances.

3. They don't actively listen to prospects
A business developer who talks more than she listens, will always struggle to close sales. Active listening is the best way for salespeople to overcome objections that stand in the way of a sale and show how the services you offer are the best fit for the prospect.

4. Prospects do not perceive your salespeople as trustworthy.

Salespeople will never be able to close if they can't build trust with prospects. If your business developers are jumping immediately into sales mode without taking time to invest in the relationship, the conversation will be short. Focus on having genuine conversations where they learn about the prospect and their needs. After that, the selling becomes easy.

5. They don't know how to close properly

Closing is an art that requires emotional intelligence, judgment, timing and a skill set that isn't taught in engineering, architecture or planning school. If you want to avoid the cost of "professional visitors" and get the benefits of strong closers, it's time to invest in some training in these vital skills.

6. Your salespeople don't have 'Drive'

The best salespeople always possess three character traits: They have a strong need to achieve, they are highly competitive, and they are unshakable optimists. These three characteristics combine into what we call 'Drive' and create an unstoppable selling machine. If your salespeople don't possess these three elements of Drive, you might be trying to push the proverbial string and nothing you do will change the situation.

   If your business developers are doing more visiting than closing, it's because their skills are lacking, the process is flawed or that all-important Drive is missing. Assess all three and then do something about it.

Are your professional services being commoditized?

There's sure no end of whining when it comes to the commoditization of professional services: Clients selecting on low price, rampant fee competition, procurement by the Purchasing Department. Why aren't clients smart enough to see the incredible value you bring?

Here's why. It's not the client's job to see value. It's our job to show it. It's our job to deliver higher value that's worth a higher price. And we're not doing a very good job in either case.

I watched an interesting video recently: a performance comparison test between a Jaguar E-Type and an Aston Martin DB5. Both were 1965 models. Both were the supercars of their day. The test revealed impressive acceleration, handling and braking from each car and collectors today line up to pay hundreds of thousands when they come available.

Then the testers brought out a new, bone-stock, base model Honda Civic. And it completely smoked those two iconic cars in every performance indicator. The bar is constantly being raised. And if you want to stay ahead of the commodity wave, you have to raise your game accordingly.

There is nothing about our status as a 'professionals' that excuses us from the fray and scrabble of the regular business world. We're selling 'stuff' into the marketplace and we're subject to all the foibles and machinations of the market just like everybody else.

Sure, we pride ourselves on quality and service. But quality and service have long since become expected by clients. Without those, you aren't even invited to play in the game. In other words, they've become commodities.

Here's a revealing exercise: Take a few minutes and compare your website with those of your main competitors. Does yours really say anything different?

Here's some actual copy from an actual engineering firm's website.

> X is a consulting engineering firm, specializing in the Y fields. X is an engineering firm that is focused on identifying opportunities and providing solutions for improved reliability and efficiency. Our staff is comprised of engineers and technical experts with Y experience. We've been there and understand the challenges you go through. We have the experience and resources to support your project needs from conception to start-up.

And then X complains that their clients won't pay premium fees. Why should they!?

On the other hand, maybe you should consider embracing the whole commodity thing. Sam Walton's six heirs have a combined net worth of just under $150 billion. That's about the same as the combined net worth of one-third of the entire US population. All from selling commodities. The key is simple: Low profit margins and high sales volume.

But if you **don't** want to attend the Walmart School of Business, you have to provide clients with a clear added value for which they're willing to pay a premium.

When was the last time you raised the bar for yourself? When was the last time you introduced new services, new capabilities, new features, new levels of customer service? If you don't focus on, and regularly update that which makes you special, you're sliding down the slippery slope to commodity.

It's not the client's job to see value. It's our job to create, communicate, and deliver it.

First, we fire all the marketers…

Then we fire all the Principals.

Radical? Undoubtedly. But it's these two groups that I find are typically responsible for the mediocre marketing that goes on. Now, before the lynch mob forms, let me explain why these otherwise wonderful folks are letting us down in a big way.

Firm Principals take their jobs and their responsibilities seriously. They're accountable for the firm's success and that means winning a steady supply of profitable work. But, and I know this from personal experience, there is more time spent in engineering and architecture schools learning about the signs of the zodiac than there is spent learning about marketing. In other words, most firm Principals know diddly-squat about marketing theory or practice.

Over their careers, many have acquired some truly flawed notions and picked up a boatload of horrendous habits in the area of marketing and sales. But since their name is on the door, they somehow feel obliged to have all the answers. I've seen far more than my share of simply awful decisions being implemented because that's what the Principal believed should be done.

I'm sure you've heard the expression, 'Seldom right, but never in doubt…'

And what about the Marketers? Well these folks DID go to marketing school. They learned the theories and analyzed the case studies. If anybody knows how to sell refrigerators at the North Pole, it's these guys. But they never went to engineering or architecture school. And, in the minds of many Principals, that disqualifies them from having a legitimate opinion about how things ought to be done. Too often, the result is a glorified secretarial pool that shows up with a blank steno pad and asks the boss what they want done.

Now, in far too many cases, those Principals are right. I've mentioned that I had a chief proposal writer at a construction company ask me once, "What is design-build?" After I got back up off the floor we launched a series of 'learn-about-construction' classes for the entire marketing department.

How can you possible market or sell something about which you know so little? And how can you expect a Principal to listen to your advice when you haven't earned their trust?

Principals and Marketers need each other. Desperately. But first they need to respect each other's knowledge and talents. Principals need to sit quietly and listen to what might at times seem like wild and crazy ideas. They need to recognize that there's a body of knowledge – let's call it the 'art of persuasion' – that can guide us to winning more work.

Marketers, on the other hand, need to earn the trust of the professionals whose work they're asked to sell. Most firms desire to be a trusted advisor to their clients. Marketers should have the same goal. But trust doesn't automatically come with a degree or a designation. It has to be earned slowly, over time.

None of us know what we don't know. But with a little patience, open-mindedness and curiosity, we just might discover that there's a colleague sitting down the hall who knows exactly what you don't know. And they're playing for the same team.

Left brain, right brain – let's go marketing

Every time I land safely in an airplane and every time I make it to the far side of a bridge I say a silent one in thanks for all the wonderful engineers in the world and their fabulous, left-brained thinking. I have enormous admiration and appreciation for the logic and the discipline required to be an engineer.

But when it comes to persuading a client to buy your services, a larger dose of right brain would go a long way.

Engineers think, and have been trained to communicate in ways that are logical, factual and rational. A well-written technical paper, for example, lets the reader evaluate the facts and not be influenced by hype, opinion or emotion. But when these communication techniques are used in proposals and marketing materials you risk boring and even alienating all the non-technical, non-engineer types who might be making important decisions about hiring you. Not everybody thinks like an engineer.

In fact, the population has a broad spectrum of communication preferences. Cognitive Psychology is an entire science devoted to studying how people take in information, process it, and reach decisions. And the non-technical people of the world communicate and understand best, not through the sorting of facts and data, but through stories, allegory, examples and – yes – emotion.

It's a bit of an over-simplification, but it's quite safe to say that communication preferences are linked to the four basic personality types:

The person who values intellect needs to understand your logic.
The person who values feelings needs to perceive your motives.
The person who values stability needs to know it has been tested.
The person who values courage needs to hear you speak of action.

The best writers, speakers and presenters speak to each of these four people every time they attempt to persuade. Putting something into your proposal or presentation for each of them broadens your conversation and makes it easier for each individual to positively connect with you.

Most of us attempt to persuade as though everyone makes decisions according to the same criteria we use. Read the lyrics of a Bob Dylan song and it's pretty apparent that this guy ain't an engineer! Now read an excerpt from any recent proposal from your firm. Is it any wonder you're not winning poetry contests?

People don't all communicate in the same way. Learn to speak to all four preferences and your voice will carry rich, persuasive harmony.

You'll see it when you believe it

I f one advances confidently in the direction of his dreams, and endeavors to live the life which he has imagined, he will meet with a success unexpected in common hours.

Henry David Thoreau

There are so many complex factors involved in a successful marketing and sales program. And every day we spend hours and hours agonizing over each one. Is our firm strongly positioned against the competition? Do we have the right service mix? Have our brand building efforts reached the right audience and conveyed the right message? Have we analyzed the go/no go decision correctly? Did we stress the right issues in our proposal? Did our interview resonate with the review panel?

Every one of these considerations is important and I've spent a career studying, refining and teaching the most effective ways to master each one.

But in all the work I've done and in all the firms I've worked with over the years, there is one factor that has been present in every single event that we've characterized as a 'win.' And one factor that has been consistently missing in the losses.

That factor is a deep-rooted, unwavering belief, an unshakeable confidence that you will succeed.

When that kind of belief is present, I've seen astounding accomplishments. Without it, the surest thing can vanish before your eyes. If you do not believe, in the very depths of your soul, that you will succeed, if you allow even the thinnest wedge of doubt to push itself into your awareness, you falter and fall short of the goal.

Many of the wins I've witnessed have appeared to be miraculous – overcoming crushing odds to emerge on top. I once watched a tiny little firm of five people beat out 47 other firms – big-name, national firms from across the country – on a high-profile project they had no business pursuing. They didn't have horsepower, a massive resume or a big-time reputation. What they DID have was a completely unreasonable and unshakeable confidence that they could do it. And a singular belief that they deserved to win.

Olympic athletes know it. Successful business people know it. Breakthrough scientists know it. When you confidently, fervently and unwaveringly believe, to the very depths of your soul, that you will succeed, inexplicable forces come to your aid. The right people show up. The right connections are made. The right idea floats into your mind. And winning becomes inevitable.

"Until one is committed, there is hesitancy, the chance to draw back. Concerning all acts of initiative (and creation), there is one elementary truth, the ignorance of which kills countless ideas and splendid plans: that the moment one definitely commits oneself, then Providence moves too. All sorts of things occur to help one that would never otherwise have occurred. A whole stream of events issues from the decision, raising in one's favor all manner of unforeseen incidents and meetings and material assistance, which no man could have dreamed would have come his way. Whatever you can do, or dream you can do, begin it. Boldness has genius, power, and magic in it. Begin it now."

William Hutchinson Murray
Author of The Scottish Himalayan Expedition

Should we hang them?

A very good friend of mine is the Marketing Director for a mid-sized engineering company. Last week, in a fit of entirely unreasonable expectation, the firm committed to preparing and submitting seven proposals. That's right, seven proposals in a five-day week, produced by a marketing team of just three people. And one of them was for what is likely the largest project in the firm's history.

Now I can hear many of you saying, "Yeah, so what!?' We crank out seven proposals over lunch!"

But as with many of mankind's questionable accomplishments, just because we can, does it mean we should?

Because in the all confusion and stress of producing seven important documents, with seven different Project Managers, for seven different agencies, each with different submittal requirements, predictably, a ball was dropped. One of the agencies required seven hard copies and one electronic copy. While the hard copies were faithfully delivered, the electronic copy fell through the cracks. Non-responsive. Disqualified.

Have you ever been witness to a car accident that you saw coming long before it actually happened? Where all you could do was wince because the crumpled metal and broken glass were inevitable? If you could rewind the tape there would be plenty of opportunity and ways to avoid the hit, but once all the variables were in play, all you could do was wait for the crunch.

Not surprisingly, my friend and his small marketing team took it in the ear. And, having agreed to turn out the seven, they are guilty of failing to deliver on a commitment. But in what world is it a good idea to even ask for that kind of commitment, let alone give it? Both ends of that agreement had guaranteed failure written all over them.

I've written here extensively about how important a rigorous Go/No Go decision making process is. And one of the critical questions to ask in that process must be, 'Do we have the time and resources to produce a high quality proposal?' If the answer is a clear 'No,' then you should take a pass.

Yes, there are opportunities that you'd love to take a swing at. No, you wouldn't like it if one of your competitors took that project instead of you. But projects are like buses – there's another coming along in five minutes. And there's a limit to your ability to turn out high quality work. And when that limit is passed, it's easy to predict disaster.

I believe it should be harder to get a 'Go' than a 'No Go.' I believe Project Managers and Business Unit Leaders – and yes, Marketing Directors – should have hit rate as part of their annual evaluation. I believe that seven, high quality proposals by a team of three in one week is impossible.

The average hit rate across the architecture and engineering professions is about 25% to 30%. So submit 10 proposals, win two or three. If you were to submit just five, you'd still win the same two or three, but you'd get a little more sleep and probably be home for dinner, too.

But here's the funny thing – if you only submit five, you'll have time to get them done the way they should be done, and you'll probably win three or four.

Your choice.

Nailed it!

G ot an email from a valued client last week.

"We nailed the presentation last Thursday, and just got the call that we are selected. The caller indicated that the committee's choice was clear; early consensus achieved with very little discussion. This is a really important project for us."

This win had nothing to do with luck. It was carefully planned, strategically pursued and confidently predicted. Let's deconstruct how it came about.

The firm headed into this competition with two distinct strikes against them. First, while they'd worked with the client before, it had been infrequently and on projects much smaller and less significant than this one. Second, the client is a very large institution and the firm's resume is largely about working in the private sector. AKA, The Dark Side. Oh, and just for fun, their main competitor was extremely well known.

The firm had been tracking the project from long before the RFP was issued and throughout the pursuit, the firm Principals used their network connections to position themselves strongly and ensure they were sensitive to the high profile politics surrounding the project.

Once shortlisted, they didn't set out to duplicate the contents of their proposal in a presentation. Instead, they brainstormed about the one, single, overriding thought that they wanted the committee to take away from the interview and focused exclusively on that.

In this case it was the fact that the client was unfamiliar with the complex rezoning process required. Get it right and the project will sail smoothly for the next 20 years. Get it wrong and it's rocky shoals everywhere. The firm was supremely confident in their ability but rather than run down a long list of projects on which they'd been successful, they told three stories. Three engaging and interesting stories about success. Stories with interesting twists and turns but ultimately with happy endings.

It felt risky for them to stay away from the 'history of our firm' slides, and the 'let us tell you about our branch offices' slides, but the team was confident that they knew exactly what the client needed to hear.

While they had close to half a dozen people at the interview, it was the Project Manager's show. He led the discussion, he introduced his 'guests' and he moderated the discussion. No 'whack-a-mole' popping up and down here.

And they rehearsed. Yes, like you, every one of them had given dozens, maybe hundreds of presentations before. But never this one. By the time they walked into the interview not one of them needed bullet points on slides for crib notes. They were smooth. They were polished. They were enthusiastic. They were confident. They were winners.

While I was honored to play a small part in crafting this presentation, full credit goes to the team. They were willing to toss out conventional wisdom and take a risk by putting all their chips on the square they knew was the client's biggest challenge. Sure there were other issues, but focusing on that one made the presentation clear, succinct and memorable.

It ain't you we're trying to persuade

Funny thing about persuasion – one size doesn't fit all. And yet we continue to act as if the only size that matters, the only size available, in fact, is the one that fits us. Here's what I mean.

We all understand, at least intellectually, that different people have different world views and that what appeals to you likely won't appeal to me. You want to visit Boston because you've always dreamed of watching the Red Sox face off against the Green Monster at Fenway Park. I visit Boston because I'm fascinated by its history. Pretty basic so far.

But here's the tricky part. When we're attempting to persuade someone, we generally feel uncomfortable using the argument that appeals to the other person. We're far more at ease using the argument that would appeal to us. After all, who wouldn't want to watch the Red Sox play at Fenway!?

Actually, it turns out there are plenty of people who wouldn't cross the street for it, but if you're a diehard BoSox fan, it's hard to imagine that and even harder to create a sincere and empathetic appeal to the history buff. Without a conscious and considerable effort, we default to talking about those things that resonate with us and then wonder why that prospective client wasn't moved by your eloquence. Here's what it can look like:

What the client says about the finished project:

"The athletic field is the fulfillment of a Mayor's promise, a home for a championship team, and a place for young athletes to be engaged in team sports, stay out of trouble and have fun."

How the design firm describes the same project:

"Installed underdrainage under the field to convey runoff to

large collector pipes located several feet below grade where percolation rates were adequate."

We're uncomfortable because it can feel disingenuous or even manipulative to adopt someone else's viewpoint in the attempt to sell. If you don't feel it in your heart, how can you be authentic and excited when you're talking or writing about it?

But marketing requires us to tell a story that will resonate in the soul of the person hearing it. It can't be a story about what you, the seller, believe. It's not you we're trying to persuade. It has to be about what your prospective client believes, what matters to them, what fuels their dreams.

I've had plenty of conversations with technical professionals who respond to a marketing initiative with, "But, I don't like it." My invariable response is, "So what? It's not you we're trying to sell to."

Persuasion requires that you tell a story that's true for the person hearing it. It's not about simply sharing what you, the seller, believe. It's about what she, your listener, your prospect, your future client believes and holds dear.

Because even if you care for neither baseball nor history, Boston has great shopping. And art galleries. And music.

Measuring your marketing ROI

Many CEO's and CFO's ask hard questions about the spending of scarce dollars in the effort to win new work. And so they should! As much as the marketers might squirm under the spotlight, the questions are legitimate and need to be asked. If spending can't be justified with a clear return it should be cut off.

That said, marketing ROI is a slippery pig to grab hold of since it's usually hard to assign clear credit to any particular project win.

That new client may have first heard of your firm from an award you won, then learned more about you through your email blast program, been impressed as one of your team members spoke at a conference, then made the final decision when your well-written proposal was competitively priced. While each of these initiatives contributed, it's impossible to allocate precise percentages of effort that resulted in the win.

There's an old saying in the ad business: "Fifty percent of all advertising works. We just don't know which half." While I know more than a few technical professionals whose hair might catch on fire from this notion, there are still some guidelines that will help you get the most from your marketing dollars.

Here are the four measures that I like to use:

1. Do you have a marketing plan and is it being executed on schedule? If you have a solid marketing plan and it's being rolled out relatively close to schedule, you WILL see results from your efforts. Think of it like a fitness program – if you're eating properly and exercising daily, you are getting more fit, whether you weigh yourself every day or not.
2. Is 'brand awareness' increasing as measured by client surveys? When you survey your target market, using whatever survey

techniques are appropriate, do you learn that more prospective clients know about you and would be willing to give you a try?

3. Are you receiving positive, informal feedback? Your senior executives, project managers and business developers ought to be seeking regular feedback from clients in their day-to-day engagements. A simple, 'How are we doing lately?' or 'Is there anything we could be doing to improve our service to you?' at every encounter will give you plenty of informal feedback.

4. Are your hit rates increasing? This includes click rates on your web site and win rates on your proposals and interviews. These should be tracked carefully and you ought to be seeing steady and regular improvement.

For sure, the diehard left-brainers in the group might find the lack of multiple decimal places unnerving. And it's certainly possible to analyze the ROI on specific efforts in a more fine-grained manner. But I believe that, for the most part, these four measures, only two of which produce actual numbers, are all you'll need to measure the effectiveness of your market efforts.

Can you see it?

I had a fascinating day last week as we attended the annual shareholders meeting of Tesla, the electric car company founded by billionaire entrepreneur, Elon Musk. The business portion of the meeting lasted no more than five minutes. The interesting part, about four hours as the multi-talented Mr. Musk told stories about the early days of Tesla, the big ideas, the failed experiments, the almost-went-bankrupt nail-biters and the incredibly successful phenomenon that continues to unfold as this still-new company rewrites the rules on personal transportation.

Turns out that Elon is a truly terribly public speaker, a reasonably talented engineer and a stunningly brilliant visionary. And there's the key. In story after story he told us that he could see the end results in his mind's eye. He readily admitted that, at many points he didn't have a clue as to HOW he would actually get to that end result, but he didn't for a moment doubt that he would.

I love reading about and speaking with successful entrepreneurs. And the one thing they all have in common is the ability to visualize the goal they are heading towards.

For example, I just finished reading a great book by Daymond John, the entrepreneur founder of the FUBU clothing line and multimillionaire member of the team of Sharks on the popular TV reality show *Shark Tank*. The book highlights both his own experience and that of a number of other successful entrepreneurs as they founded and built their companies. And in every case, the driving force was the clarity of the vision they each had for what they wanted to accomplish.

So, when you look out into the future of your firm, what do you see? Can you describe a detailed picture of where you'll be and what you'll be doing? What projects will you be working on? What clients you'll be serving? Can you visualize this day three years from now?

Notice that I'm using words that all talk about vision, pictures and seeing. The reason this is so important is that it forces you to have tremendous clarity about your goals. If they're the least bit vague or clouded, the likelihood that you'll achieve them falls off rapidly.

So when you think about your firm 36 months, 1,080 days from today, what color will the walls be? What window will you be looking out? What client will you be calling? What will the top and bottom line on last month's financial statements say? How will this picture be different from the one you see today?

Like Elon Musk, you might not have a clue about how you're going to get there. But that's not nearly as important as knowing where you want to get to. You'll figure it out, bit by bit, along the way.

When you drive at night, the headlights on your car illuminate only the few hundred feet in front of you. But you can drive from Seattle to Miami seeing only that much at a time. You don't need to see the whole route, but you do need to see Miami in your mind.

Daymond John makes a great comment near the end of his book that is going to stick with me: "You can't hit a target that you can't see."

What does your target look like?

How to suck the life out of a project

Your firm pours its heart and soul into the projects you do. They become your pride and joy. You brag about them to friends, you drive your kids past them on weekends. For all I know, you probably show pictures of your projects to your Mom. All of which is fantastic because it reflects the well-justified pride you take in the work you do.

But then it comes time to write descriptions of those projects. Descriptions that are used in your proposals, on your website, in your brochures and SOQs. And in that process we suck the life from them and turn them from game-changing miracles into shriveled up, lifeless carcasses.

Sound harsh? Let's look at some examples. In each of the following actual cases I've taken finished projects and compared what the client has said about the job on their website against how the firm describes the same project on theirs.

On their website, the city describes the new park as, **"…a picturesque swath of green to the heart of the city. The fountain, close enough for adults to touch and children to run through."** You can almost hear the kids squealing in delight from here!

The firm, however sees the project as, **"A fully integrated set of construction documents and coordination of the utility work and technical approvals for the project."**

The communications company says their new data center will, **"Help companies accelerate business performance by connecting them to customers and partners inside the world's most networked data centers. It's a strategic communications hub for the eastern United States and a major communications gateway to Europe."** Talk about thinking big!

The firm? It sees only **"A Zoning Conversion and Special Exception permit; topographic and construction surveying,**

141

high accuracy building control for construction, easement plats and utility mapping, preliminary engineering including stormwater and sanitary sewer and water trunk lines, a concept grading plan and roadway design."

The library's website positively gushes as it invites patrons to get involved with the building's ongoing performance: **"...energy production, energy consumption, the weather at the center and many other parameters can be viewed at the online smart building kiosk. Many of the design features that make this center a model for energy and environmental design can be viewed in the "green features" section of the kiosk."**

The firm's description, on the other hand, could put you to sleep. **"The complex includes approximately 20,000 SF of public library space and an additional 20,000 SF of administration offices. The library houses a collection of 150,000 books and periodicals and features a 15,000 SF multi-purpose community center and an outdoor amphitheater."**

Your projects have a huge impact on those who benefit from them. Entire towns enjoy clean water, corporate profits go up, neighborhoods become safer and institutions fulfill their missions more effectively. Don't ever be afraid to celebrate and take pride in the role you've played in these achievements! We're in no danger of losing the left-brain view of what this profession does. But a little more right-brain input would go a long way towards putting the life back into these miracles you manifest every day.

Get with the program!

Had lunch with an old friend today. He's been a lawyer for almost 40 years and we both know some recent law graduates who are being admitted to the bar this year. My friend was recalling how, when he was called to the bar, he was required to take an oath to never engage in 'champerty and tout.'

Yeah, I had to look them up too.

Champerty is when a lawyer agrees to take on a case and, if successful, receives a percentage of any settlement. In other words, it's the basis of every contingent fee lawsuit today!

A tout is someone who solicits business in a persistent and annoying manner. In other words, every lawyer with a billboard, a bus stop ad or those annoying TV ads asking if you've been injured.

My, how times have changed for lawyers!

And they've changed for other professionals too. It wasn't that long ago that you'd get your professional wrist slapped if you even contemplated advertising or promoting your services. Restrained word of mouth was king and we went to great lengths to cut down any tall poppies, ensuring that everyone toed the line.

My, how times have changed for professionals!

While the designation 'professional' is complimentary, there are so many professionals in business today that fierce competition is rampant and the polite world of four decades ago is just quaint. The truth is, we sell stuff into the marketplace. And the stuff that we sell is just as subject to the pressures, machinations and foibles of the marketplace as it is for the average dry cleaner, retail store or car repair shop.

However, your 'professional' designation continues to hold you to a higher standard of performance than the average dry cleaner or retail store.

But that doesn't buy you a pass when it comes to aggressively promoting your firm, using every means available. In addition to the normal relationship-building efforts of our business developers, firms today have to embrace advertising, public relations, email marketing, social media, content marketing and every other tool that's available in the promotional toolbox.

The concept of and need for a strong 'brand' has arrived for professionals and it's vital that your firm embrace it. It's simply no longer enough to promote your firm on the merits of the work you do. Everybody does good – even great work. The incompetent and the merely adequate have been weeded out and the competitors you face – the ones who want to eat your lunch – are damned good at what they do. Without a strong promotional program that is specifically designed to build your brand image across your target market, your firm is going to be trampled by the firms who have decided that our versions of champerty and tout can be profitable ideas. Bemoan the loss of innocence if you want. But stand aside while you do because you're about to be run over.

Your presentation needs road signs

Y ou've seen him—the presenter who speaks so fast you can't tell where one thought stops and the next begins. In fact, it often seems as if that type of presenter has never encountered a comma or a period in their life!

When you read a book you're used to it being divided into chapters, paragraphs and sentences. You rely on periods, commas, paragraph breaks, subject headings and chapter titles to signal that you've finished reading about one topic and are about to switch to a different one.

But when you're giving a presentation, how does your audience know when you've finished one thought and are moving on to the next? They know because you're going to put 'road signs' in your presentation that will show your audience where you're going and keep them informed of progress along the way.

Early in your presentation, give your audience a very brief verbal agenda: "Today I'm going to show you the four keys to success on this project." As you say "four keys to success," hold up four fingers of one hand so they get a strong visual of the number four. Then they can keep a mental count of where you are as you move through the presentation.

Be conscious of speaking at a slow, steady pace. I don't want you to sound monotonous, but too many speakers let their jittery nerves turn into a high-speed mouth with nary a pause as words fly at 100 miles an hour. It can be fun watching these presenters slowly turn blue from lack of oxygen as they fail to even take a moment to breathe!

When you reach the end of a thought, pause and take several breaths. This signals the audience that you're about to switch to a new topic. It also gives you a chance to collect your thoughts, relax and get ready for the next section.

At first a pause like this will feel awkward; we always feel like we should fill in any silence. Radio broadcasters call it 'dead air.' But if you listen to a talented speaker - watch some clips of Ronald Reagan or Bill Clinton - you realize that they pause frequently and the silence is not the least bit uncomfortable. In fact it adds to the quality of the presentation and to our ability to follow and understand.

When you're ready to move to the next section - say the third key to success - announce that you're moving on while holding up three fingers to remind them of your first road sign and give them an update on your progress through the presentation.

You can also put road signs into your slides. If you want to pause and have some dialogue or speak in a little more detail about a particular topic, put in a blank slide that is just black. This will let your audience focus on you instead of the slides.

Pausing, gesturing, announcing and showing by way of your slides: these techniques replace the all-important punctuation and spacing that guide us through a text document. And they provide invaluable assistance to your audience as they try to follow you.

You don't need more proposals

You need better ones.

Have you ever watched one of those tractor pull competitions? A farm tractor has to pull a heavy sled as far as it can down a dirt track. So far, a pretty simple task. But someone with a twisted sense of humor designed the sled so that, as you move down the track, the weight on the sled moves forward, making it harder and harder to pull. In other words, the further the tractor pulls the sled, the more difficult the task becomes. Ultimately, it's impossible to move the sucker and you stop.

It's a game in which everyone inevitably loses. The winner is the one who loses last.

Which brings me to proposal writing. A disturbingly high number of firms act on the premise that, the more proposals we submit, the higher the likelihood that we're going to win something. As with the tractors that have been modified to have two, three and even four engines, the thinking is that high volume and high horsepower can win the day.

But invariably, as your proposal volume goes up, the quality goes down along with your chances of winning any given project. The harder you try, the less likely it is that you'll come out on top.

How bad does it get? I've met firms that are submitting more than a thousand proposals a year! Since there are about 260 working days in a year, that's almost four proposals a day. Two every morning, and two more before you go home. Repeat tomorrow. And these aren't even the mega-firms with thousands of employees and big marketing departments! These are ordinary firms with ordinary resources.

The average hit rate for proposal success in the design professions is between 25% and 30%. Write 10 proposals and win two or three projects. But what if you decided to only write five proposals? It would be pretty easy to rank the ten opportunities in order of most-to-least likelihood of winning. Then simply eliminate the bottom five.

You're still going to win the same two or three that you would have won before. But now you've cut your proposal workload in half and doubled your hit rate. Since writing losing proposals is pure overhead cost, you'll also save yourself a pile of cash and reduce your stress.

But something even better happens too. Suddenly you've got twice the time and twice the resources to put into the five proposals you've chosen to write. More time to research. More time to develop a win strategy. More time to customize your response. More time to write and edit well.

As you can easily predict, instead of writing five and winning two or three, suddenly you'll be writing five and winning three or four. One simple move that makes your life easier, cuts your overhead costs, reduces your stress and increases the number of projects you win.

Try it!

The scourge of the urgent

I took a vacation recently and used the time to catch up on some reading that I've been wanting to get to. While there may have been at least one trashy novel involved, there were also some inspiring books by people I admire.

My biggest take-away was that I spend way too much time spinning my wheels, dealing with the urgent instead of the important. This isn't a new concept but I'm grateful for the slap-in-the-head reminder.

We all have to-do lists that fill our days. Most of us, though, have more list than day and we compensate by cheating ourselves as we give up sleep and leisure time, cheating our families by stealing time that rightfully belongs to them, cheating our clients and customers by doing a less-than-excellent job on the work we've agreed to take on. Or all three.

But the truly wise have found a different way. A far more successful, elegant and satisfying way. They simply refuse to do anything that won't take them a giant step forward towards the important goals they've set for themselves.

As much as that sounds revolutionary, insubordinate and irresponsible, it's supremely intelligent and sane.

It begins with knowing what you want to accomplish. By setting goals for yourself, your team, your firm. And then plotting a course that takes you on the straightest line from where you are today to where you want to be. Anything that causes you to step off that line is a distraction and a waste of your precious time.

Way back in 1994, Jim Collins and Jerry Porras wrote their seminal book, *Built to Last: Successful Habits of Visionary Companies* and introduced us to the concept of the Big Hairy Audacious Goal. But BHAGs don't just apply to companies. They are just as important to individuals and teams.

What are you trying to accomplish? Where are you going to be one year, three years from now? If you were just one day away from that amazing accomplishment, what would be the second-last thing you'd do? What is the step before that? And the one prior to that? If you regress all the way to today, what would your to-do list look like as the first step towards that goal? My bet is that it would be different than it is now.

Here's a hint: if the deadlines for the items on your to-do list are mostly less than a week away, you're working on urgent, instead of important things. If, however, those deadlines are several weeks, a month, or six months out, you're focusing on the things that are going to take you to exciting new places.

As wheels spin and dust flies, it's easy to kid ourselves that we're getting work done and accomplishing things. But the real measure is in your progress towards those life-changing goals that you've set for yourself.

Look around. If the scenery is the same as it's been for as long as you can remember, you might want to check your to-do list.

Your fees aren't too high

The MSRP for a brand new Lamborghini Aventador is $402,295. If that's a little more than what you'll find between the sofa cushions right now, you can lease one for just $6,692 per month.

What kind of a car sells for almost half a million dollars? One that can get to 60 mph in just over two seconds and tops out at well over 200.

A few weeks back, I was on the freeway outside one of our major cities with one of these supercars right on our tail. In the rush hour traffic, he was going the same 5 mph as we were in our rented Kia Optima.

So why would anyone choose buy a car that, in all legal traffic situations, can't outrun an econobox? For a price that would buy you 18 Kias? Because they perceive that the value they get is worth more than the money they have to trade for it.

This is a fundamental rule of economics and pricing: Regardless of the price point, as soon as a customer believes that the value they receive is greater than the money they must part with, they'll buy.

I hear so many firms today bemoaning the fact that fee competition is so red hot rampant. That clients are price shopping all the time, fees are being undercut and desperate firms are buying projects. The problem, though, isn't that your fees are too high. The problem is that the value you're selling is too low.

No client wants to buy the services you sell. No matter what you do, you won't ever convince a client that the ability to size a pump, design a beam or manipulate square footage is worth what you want to charge.

In the process of selling, we need to use more than just facts. We need to appeal to a deeper, more personal place than just logic. We need to focus on the benefits and the value they will get <u>after</u> you've done your work. Clients don't want civil engineering, they want a reliable waste treatment plant that can handle their growth. They don't want architectural services, they want the prestige that a new city hall is going to bring to their municipality.

Clients have two things on which you need to focus if you hope to persuade them of the value you bring: They have problems and they have desires. The more problems you can identify and help them solve (whether identified in the RFP or not) the higher your value. The more desires you can help them achieve, the more willing they are to pay your fee.

But too many firms focus only on the services they provide. When your competitor is willing to provide the same services for half the fee, you lose.

There is a subtle, but extremely important difference between the problems and desires of your client and the services you sell. They're happy to pay good money for the first. They pitch a fit about paying for the second.

Your job is to establish sufficient value in the client's mind. Because as soon as they perceive that the value you're going to provide exceeds the price they have to pay, they're ready to buy.

Never ask for the job

I'm willing to bet that someone, somewhere along the way in your business development training, coached you to 'always ask for the job.' At the end of a presentation, while you're socializing, whenever you're in the presence of a client with a project, you should be sure to ask them for the job.

But I'm here to tell you that that was bad advice. And further, I'm going to tell you that you should NEVER ask for the job. Let's explain…

Closing the deal is the oh-so-vital final step in the sales process. Fail to do this and the rest of the effort was wasted. So a good business developer is always looking for what we call 'closing opportunities,' those moments when the client sends out key signals that they have enough information and interest in you to make a buying decision.

What do those signals look like? Watch for body language that signals a high level of interest. Listen for verbal clues, which can be subtle. Expressions such as 'Oh?!' or 'Hmmm!' indicate a heightened interest. And sometimes they're obvious such as, 'That's what I've been looking for!' or 'Okay, I want it!' At that point, there's no need to go farther.

You create momentum towards closing opportunities by getting a series of smaller agreements from the client. At each point in your presentation or conversation, get the client to agree that the statement you've just made will help solve their problem or satisfy their desire. For example you would ask, "Would you agree that our technical approach would solve the dissolved oxygen problem you're experiencing?" Or, "Would you agree that this entryway configuration would give you the circulation you're looking for?"

These aren't rhetorical questions. Pose them, and then wait for the 'Yes,' answer. This series of agreements forms a 'Yes' pattern and builds momentum towards the final 'Yes!' But the pattern doesn't form on its own. Without these 'tie-down' questions tacked on at the end of each statement there is no guarantee you'll get them to agree.

This combination of your confident leadership and their 'yes' answers will build momentum and enthusiasm for your firm and your services. Which is exactly where you bite your tongue and keep from asking for the job.

When you ask for the project, you create a dynamic in which you're asking a favor of the client. Which makes you indebted to them and lets them believe they're doing you a solid by giving you the job. Then who's in the driver's seat when it comes to negotiating?

Instead, let your enthusiasm show you want the job. Let the level of your preparation, your energy, your determination and your tenacity make it clear that you're excited about it. But always let them do the asking.

If you do it right, you'll have them asking the favor of you. "Will you please do this project for us?" And that changes everything.

Functional or fiduciary?

It takes a lot of people to make a design or construction firm fire on all cylinders. We need Principals, Project Managers, Business Developers, Technical Experts, Administrative Staff, Marketers and more.

Each team member is aware that his or her job description includes the knowledge, skills, experience and responsibilities to get it done. But too often we put all the emphasis on the function of the job and neglect the fiduciary responsibility that comes with every position in every firm.

For example, I've met way too many Project Managers who are great at ensuring that a project is complete, accurate and has a happy client. But returning a profit? Let's just cross our fingers! Or the Business Unit Leader who is so focused on bringing work into their own department that they ignore or simply don't see the cross-selling opportunities sitting right in front of them. Or the Seller-Doer who insists that the Marketing Department throw proposals at anything that moves, without any consideration for the high cost and low hit rate.

Whether you're a shareholder or not, if you're an employee, principal, associate or any other title and stature in the firm, you have a fiduciary responsibility to the firm and your colleagues.

That means that every decision you make, every task you undertake, has to be considered from the perspective of the financial impact it has on the firm. In other words, you must always ask yourself, "Is this going to help us be more profitable?"

There's a joke that's been around this industry forever that asks what you'd do if you won a million dollars. The answer is, "Run a design firm until it's all gone." If it ever was funny, it ain't now. Margins in this industry are threadbare thin with many firms struggling to make it into high single digit percentages. In this scenario it doesn't take much to tip things into the red, with nasty outcomes for everybody.

So let's all be diligent. That means an attitude of ownership. It means taking a personal stake in the outcome and assuring ourselves that the functional aspect of our daily jobs is consistent with and supportive of the fiduciary aspect.

Sure, that new design idea might improve the project slightly. But your schematic design budget is empty so save that idea for the next project. Sure, there's a (very) slim chance you could win that project if you respond to the RFP. But could the $10 grand that you'll have to spend on the proposal be better invested somewhere else?

Each of our firms has big visions, large missions and GRAND THINGS we want to accomplish. But we won't realize any of those dreams without a steady and healthy profit margin.

The opposite of commodity

Wanna sell your firm? Then you need to figure out what it's worth. And after you've done all the easy calculations on fixed assets, receivables and work-in-progress, you'll want to tack on a little something for 'Goodwill.'

Goodwill is just what it sounds like – a measure of how much the market likes you and how willing they are to keep buying from you in the future. It's an intangible asset but your accountant will guide you: **Estimate the fair market value of all identified business assets. Determine a fair rate of return on these assets. Subtract the return from the total business earnings. Capitalize the excess earnings to determine business goodwill.** Simple, right? Then take a Tylenol.

But rather than tacking it on at the end, I suggest you think of 'goodwill' as your single most valuable asset. And let's call it something else. Let's call it your Brand.

Coca Cola values its brand at just under $60 billion. The Microsoft and Google brands dance around the $80 billion mark. And Apple's weighs in at a whopping $154 billion! In each case, there are billions of real dollars in the bank as a result of something you can't see, hear or grab hold of. Perhaps we should pay attention.

Apple's accountants will tell you that 'brand value' is **"the net present value of the estimated future cash flows attributable to the Brand."** More Tylenol. But Seth Godin does a much better job when he says that, **"A brand's value is merely the sum total of how much extra people will pay, or how often they choose, the expectations, memories, stories and relationships of one brand over the alternatives."**

Which sounds a lot like Goodwill.

So from now on I want you to think: Goodwill = Brand Value. And then set out to increase it. Increased brand value shows up in client loyalty, staff recruiting and retention, new clients and firm growth.

While it might seem that you can build your brand and your goodwill just by treating your clients and employees well and doing good work, that's not nearly enough. As I've said countless times before, everybody does that.

Most firms are well known and loved by their clients. But step outside that tight circle and name recognition usually falls to zero. A company with a strong brand is well known and respected by everyone in the entire market, whether they are a customer or not. Can you find anyone who isn't familiar with Apple? Starbucks? Coke?

So in addition to doing good work, you also have to actively promote your brand. Make noise, create buzz, generate excitement with your content marketing, social media, public relations, advertising, web presence… Your brand has to be talked about, evangelized and enthusiastically embraced by rabid fans! Then its value soars.

Because the opposite of brand (goodwill) is commodity. You buy the no-name brand because it's cheap. You pay a premium for Rolex and Prada because of the statements they make.

What statement does your firm make?

There's no need to apologize

I meet so many business developers and seller-doers who are shy or reluctant about their sales responsibilities. "I don't want to appear pushy." "I don't like coming across as a hard seller or a used car salesman."

I understand those sentiments and I, too, will never push something on someone who really doesn't want it. But right here, right now, I want you to stop apologizing for selling your services to clients

Because there's a different way of looking at this that I invite you to adopt. It's a perspective that just might revolutionize the way you think about business development.

First, think back to a project you did a few years ago. A project that was really successful, the client was happy, you made a profit and everybody walked away feeling like a winner. And make sure this project wrapped up at least two or three years ago.

Next, I want you to think about the fees you were paid. Hopefully they were decent and you made a healthy profit.

But where is that money now? Have you spent it? Do you still have any of those fees hanging around? Are you still deriving benefit from the fee that client paid? Or, are you having to find other projects in order to keep the cash flowing? My guess is that the money's long gone. It was nice while it lasted, but let's face it, that was a while ago...

Finally, I want you to think about your client. Are they still enjoying the results of the work you did? Is the project still providing returns, benefits and positive cash flow? Despite the griping they did about it at the time, I bet they can't even remember the fee they paid you. But I also bet that they're still glowing about how smart they were to do the project and to hire you to do it!

So who's the biggest winner?

The fact is that your clients ALWAYS come out ahead when

they hire you. And that reluctance you have about selling? Kinda misdirected, isn't it?!

Here's the thing – the sales process isn't something you do *to* somebody, it's something you do *for* somebody! And if you don't believe that your clients are better off after you've provided your services, you should get out of this business!

But the fact is that every client ends up with far more value than the dollar amount of the fees they paid to you. The sales process is simply one in which you show them that the value you're going to provide exceeds the price they're going to pay.

When you do that, it's easy to see that selling isn't a selfish, shove-something-down-their-throat activity. It's a means by which you can help that client act in their own best interests.

Downright noble, if you ask me.

When it all hits the fan

We all know them. They're the sorts who, after they've dropped the ball, go to great lengths to assure us it wasn't their fault and deflect the blame to some other poor schmuck. The saddest thing about this kind of person is the utter transparency of their efforts. Usually, the fault is so obvious that their efforts to duck responsibility would be humorous if they weren't so despicable.

The one thing we all have in common with this poor sap is that we screw up. Regularly. And sometimes in a really big way. What separates us is what we do after we step in the doo-doo.

Who would you rather work with: The person who makes a mistake, then tells you why it wasn't really a mistake, why it doesn't matter and why it actually wasn't their fault? Or the person who comes to you, tells you they've made a mistake (often before you find out on your own) and tells you what they're going to do to fix it? Your clients would rather work with that person too.

When you try to hide a problem you've created or deflect the blame elsewhere, the trust that others have in you disappears. But when you step up and face the music, your credibility takes a huge leap. "If she's being honest with me about this, I've got to believe she's going to be honest with me about everything." It doesn't feel very good in the moment, but the long-term benefits are enormous.

Sure it's embarrassing to screw up. We all want to appear to be perfect and our egos take a big hit when we fall short of the mark. Our first instinct is to hide and hope no one notices. But then, when someone does notice, our second instinct is to make excuses or point the finger elsewhere. Every one of these actions simply digs the hole deeper, making it that much harder to climb out in the end. As much as it goes against your survival instincts, resist the temptation to duck, cover up or deflect. It makes you look like the two-year old who covers his eyes and thinks that nobody can see him.

Your client knows you're not infallible. They know you're going to make mistakes.

When you make that inevitable mistake, that's the time to show what you're really made of. Step up right away, tell the truth about what happened, then tell what you're going to do about it. It isn't that you screwed up. It's about what you do after it hits the fan.

When you mess up, 'fess up. This is a golden opportunity to set yourself truly apart from everyone else.

Five most common marketing errors

We all shoot ourselves in the foot on a regular basis. But what I don't understand is why anyone would take the same shot repeatedly. Here are the five most common ways in which people and firms consistently get sideways with their marketing.

#5   Failure to build a brand

Most firms are loved by their clients. Repeat work rates are healthy and the clients for whom they work think they walk on water. But step outside that client circle and name recognition falls like a rock. A company with a strong brand is well known by its entire market. That means EVERYONE who might ever need to buy what you sell in the next five years, whether they're a client now or not, knows about and thinks great things about you. Which is a goldmine when you're working to keep the pipeline full.

#4   Selling on merits alone

Way too many firms base their selling strategy on what can be summarized as, "We do good work." They talk about experience, credentials and capabilities. Which is great, except that all your competitors have pretty much the same experience, credentials and capabilities as you. Today's client assumes you can do the work. That's just the ante into the game. What do you bring and what are you going to do for them beyond that?

#3   Failing to differentiate

Take a few minutes to review your website. Then review the websites of a few of your key competitors. Now imagine that the names and logos were switched around. Would there be any discernable difference? The vast majority of firms look, feel, sound and act the same as all their competitors. That's the very definition of

163

'commodity.'

#2 Lack of involvement in BD

The term 'Seller-Doer' in this profession refers to all those Project Managers, Associates, Business Unit Leaders, Principals and everyone else who is supposedly responsible for bringing in their share of work. But across the board they're much better and more comfortable with the 'Doer' part of that equation. But nothing happens till somebody sells something and if we're all standing around, waiting for someone else to do the selling, nothing's going to happen!

And the number one most common marketing mistake is:

#1 Chasing anything that moves

The primary marketing strategy for most firms is the pursuit of projects through RFP responses. And the net result is an industry average win rate of less than 30%. That means that the majority of projects that are chased turn into nothing. So stop chasing so many! The really successful firms are extremely picky about the RFPs to which they respond. And as a result, they have higher hit rates and lower marketing costs. Simple, really. Want to double your hit rate? Cut in half the number of proposals you write.

There they are. If you're innocent, pat yourself on the back. If you're guilty, you might want to reassess that pain in your foot.

Six no-no's for presenters

The opening 60 seconds of your presentation are like gold. Treat them carefully and extract the highest possible value from them.

In order to preserve the high value of your opening minute be sure to **never:**

- Open with a joke. You are a technical professional, not a stand-up comic. Although it's perfectly all right and even desirable to incorporate a few chuckles into your presentation, most people are not naturally humorous and their jokes fall flat. Opening with a joke is not professional. It's old and corny.

- Start by giving a dictionary definition of a word or phrase. This has been done so often that it's almost as old and corny as starting with, "A man walks into a bar..." People know what the words mean, they want to hear what you think about those words.

- Say, "Thank you for the opportunity to present to you this morning..." It's guaranteed to be what everyone else starts with.

- Apologize for anything. "I'm sorry we were a little late getting here." "I apologize for the poor quality of the slides." "I'm sorry for the fact that (name of important firm representative) couldn't be here this morning." There are two lessons to be learned here. First, if you had done your planning and preparation and focused on the details you would have nothing to apologize for. Second, as soon as you point out something that is wrong, you give the client a great excuse for scratching you off the list of contenders.

- Use the first two minutes to cover administrative detail. You've got sixty seconds to grab their attention by the throat and put them on the edge of their seats. Reviewing the corporate structure of your Joint Venture or pointing out where the bathrooms are does not accomplish this goal.

- Think small. Instead think big. Big, bold thoughts stir the imagination and get your audience thinking along with you. If you are truly to be thought of as the only company to tackle this project, you have to think, act and be bold.

Your Brand is NOT...

I've often heard firms saying they are going to 're-brand' themselves, when in fact they're simply coming up with a new logo. Let's talk about some things that your brand is NOT.

Your Logo

Your logo is a visual image, intended to represent the company. Like your company name, it's the thing that is (ideally) remembered with 'positive predisposition.' That's marketing-speak for, 'they like you.' But the mental associations, good and bad, that are triggered by a logo are the same ones your customers and the marketplace have learned to connect with your company name.

The real value of a logo is the instant visual association that can be garnered with just a glance. No need to read anything. No need to take time to make sure you understand. Just a quick flash of that 'swoosh' and we all know it's Nike.

Your Tagline

The same angst that is invested in logo development is also put into the creation of a company tagline. But regardless of what you write, your customers will develop their own taglines based on their assessment of your quality and performance.

By all means develop and use a tagline. But make sure your project quality, attention to detail, and customer service are consistent with it or your clients will develop one of their own to reflect your REAL brand.

What you say it is

Your brand is determined by the marketplace, not your marketing department. It is your customers who will decide what your company is best known for.

That doesn't mean you have no control. You must set out to

establish your brand. But without consistent harmony between what you promise in your marketing and what you deliver in your projects, you will never control your brand.

You can launch the most aggressive brand-building campaign ever. But that brand will always be tested and confirmed by your clients. They are the ones who get to say what your brand is all about.

Permanent

Your firm today is not what it was 10 years ago. And it's not what it will be 10 years from now. As the firm evolves, so does the brand and you need to be aware of and proactive about its evolution.

Volkswagen is a very different brand today than it was when the first Beetle was introduced to the North American market in the 1960s. Likewise with Honda and Toyota. But these companies have slowly and carefully guided the transformation of their brands from cheap economy car to world-class automobile. The marketing promises have not outstripped the product quality and we consumers have been happy to let those companies guide our understanding of their brands.

It takes hard work to build and maintain a strong brand. It's assailed all the time from many sides with competitors taking pot shots, disgruntled customers or former employees raking muck and the odd black eye when delivering a project.

But it's worth all that effort. Well-known companies such as Coke and Nordstrom count the equity of their brand as a huge plus on the balance sheet. You can get that kind of equity and value from a strong brand image too. Today would be a good day to start!

Lessons from Mickey Mouse

It takes a lot of effort to keep yourself out of the commodity game. Five minutes after you start your exciting new business, three competitors open across the street, all of whom seem happy to undercut your pricing. While this sounds depressingly like Sisyphus, doomed forever to push the rock up the hill, only to have it roll back, this is also the excitement, the challenge and the creativity of entrepreneurship.

Back in the 1920s a young illustrator penned a charming character that became known as Mickey Mouse. By combining the character with the emerging technologies of animation and sound, Walt Disney was the first to produce a cartoon with synchronized sound. *Steamboat Willie* was released in 1928 and was an immediate hit. Disney made good money. Then the competitors showed up.

Walt's strong entrepreneurial spirit wouldn't allow him to be one of many, so he made a really long cartoon and in 1937 audiences flocked to see Snow White and her seven dwarfs in the first full-length animated feature film. And more competitors came.

By the mid-1950s animated cartoons and movies had become commonplace, and Disney wanted more. This time he took his characters, combined them with 85 acres outside Los Angeles, and created Disneyland. While the world had plenty of cartoon characters and amusement parks, no one had ever seen a theme park before, and the profits rolled in.

Then, in 1970, with theme parks popping up around the country, Disney again stayed ahead of the pack by turning a day at the park in Anaheim into a family vacation in Orlando.

Since then Disney has continued to expand by exploring new ideas. Today it is feature film studios, cruise lines, real estate development, and all manner of profitable ventures. This type of continuous reinvention and business creativity has kept Disney fresh, alive, and at the forefront of business success for the better part of a century.

Interestingly, Disney's business creativity not only includes new business ventures, it is equally driven by **letting go of old ideas that are no longer viable.** Did you know that the last new Mickey Mouse cartoon was released in 1953?

Every time the competition tries to catch up, Disney brings out its creative muscle to reinvent and repackage the products and services it offers, introduce new ideas, and prune out dead wood.

When was the last time you introduced a new service? When was the last time you adjusted the services you offer to keep in tune with, or ahead of, the needs of your clients? When was the last time you stopped offering an old service because the profit margins had slipped and competition was too intense?

The million dollar fee

True story...
I was asked to help a firm that wanted help to win a particular project because it came with a fee of $1 million. They'd never won a project with such a fee and the principals were drooling all over themselves.

They'd first heard of the project more than a year before when they'd been awarded a small feasibility study that preceded it. While the study didn't pay big bucks, they understood that it could lead to the larger project. Their tactic was to use the feasibility study as a marketing opportunity to win the big prize. So they made the study better than anyone expected and the client was thrilled.

However, there's always a catch...

The fee for the study was $15,000. Their cost for this study of all studies was $60,000. Of course they were aware of the loss but weren't concerned because "what's $45,000 compared to a $1 million fee?"

Now it was time to chase the big prize. I asked about the status of the project. Was it real? Did the client have the money to build it? Everything was in place with one small exception: The bond had yet to be passed. When we got down to a realistic probability of the bond passing, the firm guessed 50/50.

Then I asked about the competition. Turns out there was one other firm in contention but since our guys had performed the feasibility study, their chances of beating the other firm were still pretty good. They guessed about 70/30.

At this point, the combined odds gave them an overall probability of winning this project of just 35%. Then we talked about profitability.

The firm was not terribly efficient and made a typical profit of eight or nine percent on their projects. But this job was both bigger than they were used to and a little out of the ordinary. There'd be a learning curve. We agreed to estimate a five percent, or $50,000 profit on the job.

At this point, a little horse race metaphor will be useful.

They'd placed a $45,000 bet on a horse

The Vegas odds makers gave it 3½ in 10 chance of winning

Unlike an actual horse race, there was no payout for 2nd or 3rd place

And, if their horse did win, it would pay out a mere $5,000.

Would you make that bet?

The end of the story?

…Sometimes fairytales do come true. The bond passed, the firm won the job and escaped by the skin of their teeth.

There is actually some logic to all this

- RFP responses
- Catchy logos and taglines
- Tweets
- Client lunches and golf games
- Web sites
- Facebook, Instagram and LinkedIn pages

There are dozens of tactics that firms make use of in the effort to win a steady supply of profitable work. But often, those tactics can appear to be a messy collection of knee-jerk reactions with little or no logic to connect them.

In contrast, a successful 'get work' effort is a holistic symphony of interconnected and harmonious elements that all play nicely together and build on each other. The whole is decidedly more than the sum or its parts.

But conceiving and orchestrating that 'whole' can be a confusing process, especially when marketing is such an inexact science. Developing a high level strategy to which all these tactics effectively contribute is critical to success. Choosing and evaluating the tactics that fit into the overall strategy is vital.

I like to break marketing into a five-phase effort, with each phase setting the stage for the next. It's then easy to think about and evaluate how the individual tools or tactics that you implement contribute to your marketing success.

Phase 1 is 'Positioning.' This is where you answer critical questions such as 'Who are we?' 'What do we sell?' 'Who do we sell it to?' and, 'What sets us apart from all the other firms that want to do the same thing?' Your position in the market changes over time and the marketing planning process helps you monitor and then proactively control your strategic position.

Phase 2 is 'Brand Building.' This is where you broadcast your presence, your capabilities and your competitive advantage to the world. Curiously, the branding phase isn't intended to win projects. It's intended to create name recognition and enhance your reputation. It simply sets the stage for the selling that will take place later on down the road.

Phase 3 is 'Business Development.' This is where you build those all-important, personal, trust-based relationships, without which no client will ever hire you. Trust is absolutely essential before any client will give you the keys to their kingdom and have the faith that you will safeguard their best interests and their money.

Phase 4 is 'Sales.' This is where the client will actually choose you over anyone else to execute this particular project. Your proposal, your presentation, your face-to-face interaction with the client in this phase will result in the win or lose of this particular project chase.

Phase 5 is 'Client Service.' This is where you deliver the project and your technical staff lives up to or disproves all the marketing messages (should we call it 'hype?') of the previous four phases. It's only after this phase that your client decides whether or not they're going to come back and do it again.

Implementing a comprehensive and cohesive marketing strategy can make a huge difference to your success. There is definitely logic behind the tactics. Make sure you understand them.

Now that's different

Biologists and anthropologists tell us that humans are hard wired to notice things that are different. Way back, when we roamed the savannah, it was important to notice the lion heading your way through the grass.

Those instincts are still with us and of great use when we think about marketing. In a sea of sameness, standing out from the crowd gives you an immediate advantage when it comes to being selected for the next project.

The economic definition of a 'commodity' is any product or service that, in the perception of the buyer, is essentially identical to that available from a competitor in every way except price. So a primary goal of all your marketing efforts is to set your firm apart from your competitors.

There are four methods that your firm can use to differentiate:

1. Demonstrate experience. This is by far the most primitive and the least effective means of distinguishing your firm from your competition. But it's also the most common. It's the 'list of projects we've done that are similar to the current project.' But every competitor has that list. If they didn't, they wouldn't be competitors. The most challenging aspect of this technique is to show that your experience is unique. More often than not, the proposals I see simply say, 'we did a project like this.'

2. Show that the process you use to accomplish a client's goals is different and superior. Today's client is sophisticated and vitally interested in the methods you use to achieve their objectives. Demonstration and explanation of your process also communicate competence and build confidence. Letting the client see 'behind the curtain' gives them a sense of belonging to the inner circle and encourages a closer bond.

3. Prove that you produce quantitatively better results. This means measuring and demonstrating improved efficiency, economy, or productivity for your client as a result of your work. This is the most effective and meaningful means of differentiating, but it's also the most difficult. (Most other industries use this method regularly. Think about two socks, one washed in the featured brand and the other in brand X.) While it's difficult, it's not impossible. Can you show that the long-term cost of operation and maintenance of facilities you design is lower than average? That your projects are granted permits more quickly than the average? That contractor's bids on your projects are more accurate than average?

4. Make more noise. Be more colorful. Attract more attention than anyone else. Geico sells discount car insurance – the identical insurance that you can buy from Allstate, Progressive, Farmers and a hundred others. In 2013, Geico spent $935 million in advertising, almost three times the average spent by the rest of the 10 biggest insurance companies. In return, Geico's premium income increased by 11.2% compared with 6.5% for Progressive, 5% for State Farm and just 3.5% for Allstate. 'Nuf said.

When I look out at the sea of businesses, I see a whole lot of sameness. Your clients see an opportunity for competitive bidding.

The last word in all marketing is differentiation. What makes you stand out?

More than just 'making it pretty'

J an Tschichold.
Remember that name for a minute at least, because he had something to say that will affect the success of your proposals.

Jan was born in Germany in 1902 and became a rather influential typographer and book designer. These aren't the folks who write the words. They're the ones who make the words appear in a manner that makes them easier to read.

What he said was, **"Readers want what is important to be clearly laid out; they will not read what is too troublesome."**

Think about that – 'too troublesome to read.' That means that you could be the next Shakespeare or J.K. Rowling, but if the physical effort of reading your words is too much, readers will simply put it aside. Exactly the same principle applies to your proposal. Regardless of the brilliance of your content, if your prospective client finds it hard to find her way through it, she'll put it into the reject pile and move onto the next one.

Have you ever turned a page, only to encounter top-to-bottom, wall-to-wall text? Seems like a lot of hard slogging to get through it, doesn't it?

Good graphic design is like good design of any sort – when it's done well we benefit, often without even noticing it. A well-designed building is easier to navigate. A well-designed treatment plant is easier to operate. A well-designed document is easier to read.

In the case of your proposal, good graphic design serves a number of purposes. First, it's simply attractive to the eye. First impressions make a difference and you want your clients to be attracted to the proposals you set in front of them.

Second, it makes it easier to access the information contained in the document. There is a physical effort involved in reading and the right choices of font, alignment and line spacing can make the difference between swimming upstream or floating with the current.

Finally, effective graphic design can guide the reader's eye to ensure that the information you present is seen and 'consumed' in the right order. Let's face it, most clients don't read your proposal cover-to-cover and there's a risk that they'll miss the good stuff. Some of what you've got to say is more important than other and good graphic design guides the reader through that hierarchy of information.

We can't begin to explore the techniques of graphic design here. For all the years you spent learning to be an engineer or architect, someone else spent as much time learning to master graphic design. And in the same way your clients benefit when they hire your expertise, you'd do well to work with an experienced graphic designer to make your proposals more accessible, more readable, and yes, 'prettier.'

Because at the end of the day, while you may be obliged to write that proposal, your client is under no obligation at all to read it.

The five obligations of a marketing department

This one might sting a little.

I see two problem areas we need to focus on. First, business leaders often feel that they know more about marketing than the experts they've hired to do it for them. A degree, a license and decades of experience as a professional do not automatically translate into expertise in how to sell those services.

Second, marketers are failing to show leadership and creativity in the role they play in their firms. Yes, I've heard all about how the boss won't let you. But it's your job to educate the boss and find a way.

I believe that the marketing staff in every firm – whether that's a single individual or an entire team – has a set of responsibilities.

1. To Learn

We must remain lifelong students of marketing. Learn how marketing really works, not just in your industry but in all industries. Because the techniques we're using to sell professional services today were in play eons ago by the people who are still selling soap, cars and timeshare condos. We need to catch up. We need to know what they know – the principles behind marketing, the psychology of persuasion. You can't sell something if you don't know how selling works.

2. To Stretch

Marketers must always be stretching and testing their ideas. When was the last time your firm tried something new and really different? Can you really call your marketing strategy 'creative?' Is it really any different from what the other guy is doing? When was the last time you tried something so different that you failed spectacularly and learned some really great lessons?

3. To Question

There is a lot of conventional wisdom surrounding professional services marketing efforts. But is all of it right? Even if it did apply at one time, does it still apply? If it's really true that it's all about relationships, how did the low-cost firm steal your long-term client? What if a lot of conventional wisdom was actually kinda stupid?

4. To Guide

When I was in charge of marketing at a big construction company I would visit all the business unit leaders in the company every single day. Sometimes I'd just stick my head in the door, sometimes it would be 15 minutes, sometimes we'd go to lunch. But every time I would use the opportunity to share something about marketing. "Here's what we're working on for you." "Here's what it's going to do for your business unit." "Here's the marketing principle behind it." I gained some really great partners with a much better understanding of how marketing works.

5. To Inspire

This is a tough, competitive and high-stress business and it's easy to get down and cry the blues over the 'misses.' Somebody needs to maintain the sunny outlook. If anybody in the company ought to be capable of and responsible for high spirits, it's those who have been trained to be inherently optimistic and creative. We need a steady supply of optimism, enthusiasm and energy. I look to the Marketing Department for that infusion.

We spend so much time wringing our hands about how to stand out. But the easiest and most powerful differentiator would be a creative, energetic and sophisticated marketing strategy that puts your company in front of a huge number of prospective clients over and over and over again. Who's going to have the nerve to be different?

Then don't

As I've noted before, Seth Godin is one of my favorite current commentators on the world of marketing.

In a recent blog Seth wrote,

"A commodity is a product or a service that no one cared enough about to market."

Just about any architecture, engineering or other professional services firm you'll encounter will tell you that they work hard at marketing. They have marketing staff, they submit lots of proposals, they have a website and a Twitter account.

But just about every firm you'll encounter is kidding themselves.

Sound harsh? I hope so. Because what passes for marketing at most firms can be summed up as consisting of **"We do good work. Please hire us."**

You cannot market based solely on the merits of the work you do. Every single one of your competitors does good work too. And they give good service. And they listen to their clients. Just like you.

If you truly wish to distinguish yourself and stand out from the crowd, you have to communicate far more than your ability to do good work. Seth goes on to say that "Marketing creates value, by combining stories, design and care." That means that you have to communicate with your target market in a way that engages, excites and inspires them. Reciting lists of completed projects will never do any of those things.

If you truly believe that the services you offer are superior to those of your competitors...

If you truly believe that clients are actually better off working with the team from your firm than anyone else...

If, in your heart of hearts, you know that you'll do a better job than the other guys...

Then it's up to you to convey that in a way that makes your clients believe it too.

Seth closes out his blog with a provocative assertion that I hope will cause you to pause for a moment and think.

"Commodities are in the eye of the producer. If you don't want to sell something that's judged merely on price, then don't."

Do this when the economy is terrible

"We're busier than we've ever been."
"Things are really going well for us right now."
"We're hiring as fast as we can."

These are actual quotes from emails and conversations I've had with firms around the country in the last month. And it's true – things are about as hopping as they've ever been and a lot of firms are riding high.

Right now, marketing is the last thing on most firm's minds because winning more work is the last thing they need.

Of course it's not always like this. Anyone who's been in this business for more than 10 minutes knows full well that we are the canary in the coalmine for the economy. The instant things start to turn down those projects will disappear like a scalded cat.

I've been around for my share of downturns and it's valuable, in the midst of a bull market, to recall what is inevitably said when things head south:

"We should have been doing our marketing while things were strong."

"A weak economy is the wrong time to be searching for new clients."

"Because we didn't build our relationships then, we're having to compete on price now."

So if these are the good times, in what kind of marketing should you be investing in order to be able to gloat when that oh-so-predictable downturn shows up?

Now is the time to be building your brand. To be expanding the visibility of your firm beyond your client list. NOT chasing RFPs. NOT trying to win projects. But building name recognition in broader markets. Enhancing your reputation. Expanding your 'mind share' beyond those clients who already know you.

If you're like most firms you're extremely well known within your circle of clients. They love you. They think you walk on water. But outside that circle, the response is usually, "Who? Never heard of them!" So right now is the time to invest in building your brand outside that tight collection of clients who know you so well.

This is also the time to be building your marketing systems. Cleaning up your libraries and databases, upgrading your systems, perfecting your processes. Build your marketing plans and infrastructure. Get your house in order so you're ready for the day when things go suddenly sour.

Because when that day comes, and you know it will, you'll be in a position to simply implement your well thought-out plan. To execute. To reap the benefits of your careful preparation.

When everyone else will be frantically scrambling and cursing themselves for failing to use these prosperous times to good effect, you'll be basking in the glow of a steady supply of profitable work. Winter is coming. Will you be prepared?

So shut up already!

We talk too much.

And we write too much.

And your clients would appreciate a whole lot less of each.

You may have noticed, a few years back, that clients started to impose page limits on proposals. That wasn't some well-intentioned effort to save more trees. It was a desperate, self-defense measure against firms who were burying them with way too much information.

In far too many firms, the selling process consists of providing clients with ALL possible information. The smarter firms, on the other hand, know that it's only necessary to provide them with enough. No more, no less.

If you've ever started a campfire you know that it begins with a match and a tiny pile of dry twigs. As the flame grows you add small sticks, then larger ones and finally the big log that will burn for hours. Dropping the log on the match is a sure way to extinguish it.

Courtship (and sales) is the same. A little information to create interest. A little more to sustain it. A little more to fan the flame of intrigue and desire. If, on your first date, your spouse had learned everything there was to know about you, things might not have turned out the way they did.

Now, in contrast to courtship, the other reason that clients began to impose page limits is because they don't actually care about you. Reading all that stuff about your founders, your branch office in Topeka and the award you won in 1987 is boring and off point.

Clients don't hire you because they love you or for the joy of working with you. They hire you to solve a problem or fulfill a desire. They are always acting in their own best interests. Your job is to show that retaining you will further that self-interest. You don't accomplish that by detailing every aspect of your firm and services. You do it by showing the benefits that the client will enjoy when you're done.

I've met firms who firmly believe that, given 20 pages on which to write, they've somehow fallen short of the mark if even one square inch of that space isn't used to provide still more information about the company, its history, its capabilities, its multiple offices, its culture, its…

If a client gives you 20 pages and you make your point in 10, they'll love you forever! I've never heard a client complain that you finished your engaging and persuasive presentation in less time than they'd allotted you.

You should write or talk until your prospect perceives that the value you're going to provide exceeds the price they have to pay. Then you should shut up because they're ready to buy.

The dirty little secret of professional services marketing

To many of the solidly left-brained geniuses who live on the STEM side of the street, a warm fuzzy subject like marketing and business development can seem like an intimidating horror house of smoke and mirrors. But the truth is that marketing is a dead-simple, logic-driven, easily-understood subject. Marketing makes calculus look like, well, calculus!

Now, for the most part, we marketers haven't wanted you to know that. Job security, you know…

But here's the deal. There are a few basic concepts that underlay any successful 'get work' program. Stick to them and it works. Quite predictably, actually. Ignore them, remember them only occasionally, or get them wrong and, even more predictably, it doesn't work.

So what are those concepts?

The first is **differentiation**. What can I get from you that I simply can't get from anyone else? The lack of differentiation is the most common mistake that most firms make. To look at the websites, read the proposals and hear the presentations you'd swear that the vast majority of firms were identical. "We do good work!" "We give great service!" Who doesn't!? But in a world of service providers who all look and sound the same, the obvious question becomes, "Who's got the lowest price?"

The second concept is **'client-centric.'** Everything you say or write must answer your client's ever-present question, "What's in it for me?" The fact that your firm has been in business for 50 years or has six branch offices is irrelevant. They want to know how their lives, businesses, egos, bank accounts, election results, peace of mind… are going to be better because they've worked with you.

The third is the simplest of all – **frequency and regularity**. Think of it like this: You've just met a nice girl or guy and you'd like to see them a lot more. Your chances are far better if you call, text or drop by with roses regularly than if you only talk on those (rapidly diminishing) occasions when you're on a date. If the only time a prospective (or past) client hears from you is when there's an RFP on the street, the relationship isn't going to last long.

Of course, God is in the details and there's a lot more to talk about. But every successful marketing and sales strategy is built on these fundamentals. And one or more are notably missing from every unsuccessful one.

Funny thing about money

The most common pushback we get when trying to sell services is that the fees are too high. The client doesn't have the money.

But the funny thing about money is that, unless one is truly destitute, we always seem to be able to pay for the things we perceive to be really important. The fact is people buy what they want if they want it more than they want the money it costs.

Now, if what you're selling is no different from what the firm down the street is selling for less, your client has a legitimate reason to turn you down. So the onus is on us to find and highlight the differences.

As marketers, as business developers, it's our job to identify the benefits you provide in addition to the basic scope of work you'll perform. It's our job to show how the benefits you provide are more valuable than the money they cost.

Do that, and the money is magically available.

You're really hard to reach!

Funny thing about being in business. It requires that you have clients.

Statistically, most firms get 70% to 90% of their work from repeat clients. These folks love you and want you to do their next job. And the next, and the next.

But even at a repeat work rate of 90% you still need a steady supply of new clients coming in the door just to stay even. And if you intend to grow…

That new client wants to get in touch with you. But way too many firms make it very hard to do so. I can't count the number of business websites I've been to that have little or no contact information. Go to the Contact page and you get a form to fill out and submit, AFTER you've convinced the robot sentry that you're not a robot.

The best firms make it easy to get in touch. They provide contact names, addresses, phone numbers and yes, email addresses. For everyone – and I mean EVERYONE – in the firm.

Of course I've heard the argument that you don't want to put email addresses on the website because a) you don't want headhunters taking pot shots at employees and b) you don't want to be deluged with spam.

Both of those excuses are pretty lame compared to the penalty you pay by putting communication barriers between you and that list of clients and legitimate business partners who want to get in touch.

If you're getting emails that you don't want, there is always an unsubscribe button at the bottom. Really simple. If you don't want employees to be snagged by headhunters, make your firm a great place to work. The employees will tell the headhunters where to go.

But please make sure that your clients and those who want to be clients can easily, conveniently and flexibly get in touch.

First, let's trash all the PowerPoint decks

We're all familiar with 'Death by PowerPoint.' We've all fallen asleep during a presentation. We've all wished for the nerve to get up and walk out rather than listen to someone read even more bullet points from their slides.

Your objective in a presentation is to connect with your audience. To engage with them in a way that gets them excited, persuades them, educates them, leaves them motivated.

The problem with PowerPoint is that it has been designed as a tool that is convenient for the presenter. It has not been designed as a tool that is convenient for the audience.

And it truly does make a presenter's life easy. It's a great tool for organizing your thoughts: Click here to add title. Click here to add text. Add a diagram. And snap! you've got a presentation. Then, to make things even more convenient, you've got all your cheat notes right up there on the screen so you don't have to remember anything. You can simply stand there and read to your audience!

But… Think again about your objective in a presentation. It's to make a personal, even an emotional connection with your audience. If you could accomplish that by simply reading your client a document, why not just send an email?

What are the dynamics of a typical PowerPoint presentation? First, everyone is sitting, facing the screen, not the presenter. Second, the presenter is either standing off in a dark corner, or standing in front of the audience but with his back to them, and everyone is reading together. The presenter out loud, the audience silently.

The best presenters, the best speakers, the best teachers and preachers know that the only way to connect with an audience is to engage them with eye contact, body language, vocal expression, enthusiasm and genuine emotion. None of those things can happen if we're all simply reading bullet points together.

Make me look good

Whenever you're preparing a proposal, particularly one that is going to any kind of highly bureaucratic organization such as a government agency or large corporation, there's an important element to address that is never mentioned in the RFP.

Whereas the owners and stakeholders in a closely held business tend to be focused exclusively on results and enjoy having the bar continually raised, the people who keep the wheels turning in a bureaucracy frequently have an additional concern that is best summed up as, "What's in it for me?"

In contrast to the risk-taking entrepreneurs in small business, those who staff large organizations tend to like the security that comes with their positions and are reluctant to rock the boat. And taking the risk to select you for this project would definitely be inviting the swells to wash over the gunwales.

Think about it: If you're not the incumbent, if you're not a well-known and proven commodity, if you represent change, whether big or small, you put me and my world at risk. To calm my nerves you need to address some important, but unasked questions.

- How will you make me look good? Will you work to have the success of this project reflect well on me to my superiors?
- If it all hits the fan and they come looking for my head, how can I defend my decision to select you? How can I avoid being blamed?
- Are you going to play by my rules? Whether I happen to like them or not, we have ways of doing things around here and I can't have you messing with that. If I need your reports by the 25th of each month, I can't have you sending them on the 30th.
- Are you going to make me work harder than I already am? I know you think that bureaucrats have an easy life, but we've been

cut back, downsized and optimized within an inch of our lives and I can't have you adding to my workload or my stress.

- Will you be challenging me or cooperating with me? While I need your expertise, I know quite a bit too and we've worked out a pretty good system here. Although it might not be exactly how you'd do it, give me the benefit of the doubt.
- What's in it for me? I don't need (or want) kickbacks or under-the-table favors but I do want to know that my life is going to be easier instead of harder, more enjoyable instead of more miserable, interesting instead of dull and that you're going to always be thinking about how things look and feel from my side of the desk.

Your client is retiring

It's been a great run. You've known each other for years and there's been a whole lotta work come from that great relationship.

But it's all coming to an end.

Unless, of course, you do something to prevent that fade-to-black.

It's inevitable that your client – meaning the individual with whom you have such a great relationship – is going to retire. Or move on to another gig. But what are you doing to preserve the steady supply of work that has come from that client's company or agency?

In far too many instances, the relationship between firm and client organization hangs on just one person. Lose that relationship and that client is history. In engineering it's called 'single point of failure' and it's to be avoided like the plague.

Right now, we're seeing a large number of key contacts in client organizations taking their gold watches and heading to the fishing hole. Perhaps you, too, are close to retirement. If you and that contact of yours are retiring soon, you need to ensure that the relationship with the client's agency or company can easily survive one or both of your departures.

You do this by nurturing additional relationships at multiple levels throughout both organizations. Of course, this is what you should be doing all along, impending retirement or not. It's vital that individuals in leadership roles have a strong relationship. But it's equally important that people at various levels of seniority in your firm develop and maintain similar relationships with their counterparts in the client's shop.

This provides you with multiple benefits. First, it reinforces the link between the two organizations. If one person-to-person relationship was to end for any reason, there are others in place to preserve the company-to-company connection. Second, it provides multiple sources of information. While you and your fellow CEO are discussing high-level strategy, the junior engineers are trading information about operations and equipment. Finally, it's a great training ground for your staff as they learn to initiate and nurture their own networks. When the day comes that the two – no longer junior – engineers are sitting in their respective corner offices, the solid relationships will already be in place.

Yes, your client is rapidly approaching the day when she hands in her key card. What are you doing to ensure that day isn't also the end of the steady work she has represented?

Six most common proposal design errors

The decisions you make about graphic design, page layout, font selection and color choice in your proposal can significantly add to or detract from a client's ability and willingness to give it the attention it deserves. Far beyond simply 'making it pretty,' effective graphic design guides the reader's eye to ensure that priority information is seen and understood.

Here are the six most common graphic design errors we see in proposals every day.

Low resolution images

Those heavily pixilated images scream 'poor quality' so loud that your prospective client is forced to put your proposal down immediately. If you can't be bothered to have high quality images in your proposal, what kind of effort are you going to do on the project?

Too many fonts

This is a classic case of 'just because you can, doesn't mean you should.' Use fonts with restraint. Pick a font family – one of the classics will do just fine – then stick to it. Create a simple hierarchy to indicate headings and subheadings, but don't get carried away with emphasis. The same font, same size but simply bolded does a fine job of indicating a section heading. A heading that's bolded, italicized, underlined and in a different color is just shouting.

No white space

I've met many technical professionals who assume that, since you have space on the page, you should fill it with content. This simply makes your document harder to read and comprehend. Give every element in your proposal room to exist. Group like elements and then add some extra space around them to pad them from other elements. This gives the reader a mental pause to digest the information before moving on to the next. Edit your text down so that you get the message into the space in a way that fits comfortably.

Too much color

Too many colors can appear cluttered, busy and informal while lack of color altogether can feel stark. Inappropriate color pairings or colors that are too strong are hard on the eyes and can even appear to vibrate when viewed. Stick to two or three colors and tints for maximum impact. If you're not sure, Google 'complementary colors' and pick a scheme that appeals to you. Colors should have enough contrast to create separation but enough similarity to create harmony.

Boring images

More photos of excavations, pump installations, empty intersections, empty buildings. Yes, those photos are accurate images of the actual work you did. But dang, they're boring to look at! You designed the building so people could use it. Show people using it! You designed the water treatment plant so people could drink clean water. Show somebody enjoying a glass of clean, cold water. Find and use stock photography if you need, but please, insert some human interest with your images!

Too much noise, not enough signal

Radio broadcasters talk about 'signal-to-noise ratio,' meaning how much of what you're hearing is actual content, versus static. A page that is too full of your firm's logo, the elements of your standard template, novelty fonts and colors and other elements that don't contribute to content is just 'noisy.' Look at every bit of ink of the pages of your typical proposals and analyze how much is signal and how much is noise. Then eliminate the noise.

The words you write aren't enough. A client will walk away from a page that is too troublesome to read. Because while you may be obliged to write that proposal, your client is under no obligation whatsoever to read it.

The engineering of touchy-feely

During a recent marketing class we got into a discussion about the differences between technical and persuasive communication.

During their training, engineers and technical professionals have been taught the ways of technical writing and presenting. Focused on facts, this style is entirely objective and purposely avoids any sense of personalization. Passive, third-person voice is the standard; opinion, metaphor and enthusiasm are actively avoided.

But when you're writing a proposal or making a presentation, and your goal is to convince a client to hire your firm, you have to muzzle that technical writer and turn the dial all the way up to Persuasive. A proposal that reads like a technical report or a presentation that sounds like the defense of a doctoral dissertation won't persuade anyone, it'll lull them to sleep.

There are two components to the art of persuasion. The first consists of intellectual agreement on the facts at hand. Techies are great at this.

The second component involves triggering an emotional conviction that leads to decision and action. It's this emotional, warm-and-fuzzy part that evades many technical folks. And even if they understand that it's important, it's about a hundred miles from their comfort zone.

But the fact remains, in order to persuade others, you must trigger that emotional response. People make their decisions because it feels right. Sure, everybody weighs the facts and objectively compares the options, but the final decision is always made in the heart, not the head.

So a great proposal or presentation, one that gets people excited and motivated to act, plucks those emotional strings. It balances the objective facts with an argument that is personal, subjective and ever so human.

If we compare persuasive communication with how we were taught to convey technical information, the problem becomes clear:

- Where technical communication focuses on impartial facts, a great persuader connects at the personal level. And if you think that a client decides solely on the facts, ask a few of them about their decision-making process. You'll hear that, after gathering all the facts, it had to 'feel' right before they'd go for it.
- Where technical communication focuses on the features of a service, persuasion tells the reader how they'll be better off – happier, thinner, richer – because of it.
- Technical communication is built on a foundation – and sometimes a mountain – of data and information. But persuasion homes in on just those few issues that matter to that particular audience. It relates those issues to the real, flesh-and-blood people to whom it matters and it shows them a better solution.

Scientists, engineers and technical professionals have been taught to bleach all the poetic language, conversational style and personal opinions from their communication. Having done that, they leave their readers buried in facts, drowning in detail and overloaded with information. Confused, annoyed sometimes, but most certainly not persuaded.

Let's learn to balance the facts with the feelings, the empirical with the lyrical. If you blend both those components into your proposals and presentations you'll have a more receptive, more attentive and more persuaded client.

Big and brass

I love Lady Gaga. And Richard Branson. And Pitbull. And Jeff Bezos. And anybody else who has the audacity, the cheek to step out and say, "Yes I can!" And then follow through on the promise they've made to themselves and the notice they've given to the world.

We are conditioned from infancy to believe in our limitations. That voice in your head never shuts up as it tells you that you've never been good with money, that you shouldn't expect too much, that people from your background can't expect those kinds of achievements. We focus on the risk rather than the upside. How often have you heard, "What's the worst that can happen?"

Have you ever, instead, when considering a new move, asked yourself, "What's the best that can happen?" Have you ever thought about Oprah's humble background, Stephen Hawking's disabilities or Henry Ford's numerous bankruptcies, and concluded that, in fact, limitations are simply excuses that reside in your head and nowhere else?

It takes enormous guts to believe in yourself and set a goal that is audacious, ridiculous and even foolhardy. It takes even more guts to ignore the chorus of voices that is more than happy to tell you what you should be doing instead, how people like you should not get too big for your britches and what will happen when it comes crashing down. But the payoff is so utterly worth it.

Oh you will fail. Of that there's no doubt.

But when a toddler lands on her chubby little butt having failed (one more time) at walking she doesn't decide to quit and we don't criticize her for falling down. If you could tap into her little brain you'd see that there wasn't an ounce of self-criticism, not one bit of embarrassment because others were looking, and not a speck of doubt that, sooner or later, if she keeps trying, she'll be crossing that room on two legs faster than Daddy can keep up.

Brick walls are everywhere and we run into them on a regular basis. Which explains the bruise on your forehead.

But here's the thing about brick walls – bruises heal and walls are finite in dimension. They have a top and can be climbed. They have ends and can be circumvented. They have bottoms that can be tunneled under.

Far too often we encounter a wall and stop. Declaring that the battle is lost. And when we do, the only thing that's lost is your belief in yourself and the opportunity to be, do or have something that you've dared to dream about. And that would be a great loss indeed.

Here's the thing about big and brass: they are utterly gender-neutral and are available to anyone.

The four major roadblocks for seller-doers

When Bob, the Seller-Doer wakes up in the morning, he knows he's facing two responsibilities: He has to get completed projects out the door and new projects in the door. More often than not, if he's got time to choose only one, he'll default to the 'Doer' side of the equation. It's a 'stay-inside-your-comfort-zone' thing.

But whether it's Bob or Marsha, the situation is the same. When the pressure's on and the 'Seller' obligations are looming, there are four major obstacles that the average Seller-Doer has to overcome.
- A perceived lack of time
- Fear of the act of selling
- Unclear expectations
- Lack of sales skills

Let's tackle each one.
- Everyone has all the time there is. We're each allotted 24 hours every day – nobody gets a second more or a second less. What separates the winners from the rest of us is how they choose to use those hours. The trick is to prioritize your responsibilities. What are the things you could do today that will most advance your career? Most advance the firm? You've heard about getting caught up in the 'urgent' vs. 'important.' Project work is urgent. Business development is important.
- Just exactly what is it that you're afraid of? What do you fear will happen if you try to sell? That you'll be rejected? There's no question – you WILL be rejected, so get over it. But it turns out that rejection is the first step towards acceptance. The best business developers have high levels of confidence in themselves and don't require the approval of others to know that what they're selling is valuable and worthwhile. If you get

rejected by one, fine. Get up, dust yourself off, and move on.

- If you're not clear what it is that your firm expects from you in the way of business development, ask! This is actually far too common and the way to resolve it is to sit down with the CEO or whoever's in charge of bringing in work and ask what they expect you to do. Get a clear idea of how much time you should be investing, any quotas regarding the number of new contacts, clients, projects or revenue you're expected to bring in. You can't hit a target that you can't see.

- There was a time that you couldn't ride a bike, throw a ball, boil water or walk upright, too. But these skills were sufficiently important that you set out to learn. You tried it yourself, took lessons, got coaching or watched a YouTube video. Sales skills are just that – another of many skills you've acquired over a lifetime of trying and mastering new things. So when are you going to decide that this skill is an important one?

You've likely heard the phrase, "Power goes to those who bring in work."

We all know that the best business developers always rise to the tops of their firms. These four obstacles not only keep Bob and Marsha from their 'seller' responsibilities, they keep them from rising to the highest levels in their firms too.

What's your point?

Before you begin getting ready for your presentation I invite you to ask yourself this question: "If I assume that they will leave this presentation remembering one thing and only one thing, what would I like that thing to be?"

Because the truth is that, at best, they'll remember one major point you made. And you need to figure out what that one thing needs to be. What is the story that needs to be told?

Never begin preparing your presentation by asking how many slides. Don't ask how many bullets per slide or what the background should be. Instead, begin with a big expanse of blank wall, a pad of blank post-it notes and a Sharpie.

Whenever I am asked to help out with a presentation, or develop a 'win strategy,' this is exactly where we begin. And then we start asking questions: "Tell me about this client and the end users." "What's keeping him awake at night?" "What drives her?" "What are the key, make-or-break drivers on this project?"

You need a process to think and to think freely— to capture any and all ideas, no matter how wild and crazy. You can capture these ideas on the post-it notes and stick them on the wall. Then you can add similar, supplementary or related ideas. You can write on more notes, stick them up, move them around, group them, rearrange them and modify them until it starts to look right and it begins to hang together as a compelling story. And a 'story' is exactly what you're trying to create.

You might be familiar with the concept of a storyboard. Moviemakers use this tool to sketch out the elements and sequence of the story they're going to tell. They create some rough visuals. It's by no means the finished product but it's a fast, flexible tool that can change easily. When you're brainstorming, identify the key points that you have to get across. What's your big idea and what are the main elements of your message?

Then answer this question: "Why should my audience care?"

When you get up to give your presentation, your audience may have just sat through five others. They've certainly got plenty on their minds and many would rather be somewhere else. If it's later in the day, blood sugar is likely low. And those folks who are texting or doodling while you're talking? Their brains have left the building.

Every single point you make must have direct, relevant importance to this audience. If you can't be completely clear as to why something's important, it's a good clue that you should simply skip over the point. It doesn't need to be made.

Remember: If you've got 10 points that you want them to remember, they'll only recall how bored they were. But leave them with one crystal clear, dominant idea and they'll hang on to it for years.

It's so much more than just the words you write

I'm a big fan of Seth Godin – a marketer and business observer who has given us so many new understandings of how we communicate.

A recent blog of his pointed out that, while humans have been around for a long time, it's only in the relatively recent past that we've developed language and, particularly, writing. So, while we rely on the written word to carry the message in our proposals, there's a lot that is simply impossible to convey with that medium.

As Seth writes,

"There are a few places where all that matters is the words. Where the force of logic is sufficient to change the moment. The rest of the time, which is almost all the time, the real issues are trust, status, culture, pheromones, peer pressure, urgency and the energy in the room."

When you're attempting to persuade a client to choose you for that project over all the other great choices they have, you'd better be ready to use more than simply the words in your proposal.

The words are good at conveying the facts – your experience, your credentials, the technical approach you'll take to the project. But they're not so good at conveying your attitude, your commitment, the passion you bring to your work, the way your team syncs as a cohesive whole.

Never underestimate the importance of those more subtle messages in the process of persuading a client. Because once they're convinced that a firm is capable of successfully executing the project, they're still left to sort out all the warm fuzzy stuff. Will this choice help my career? Are there any optics or politics that I have to consider? What's it going to be like to spend the next six months working with these people? Is this the safest choice? If things go sour, will it all rain down on my head?

Sure, you can try to answer those questions in writing, but we're never completely persuaded. We've been exposed to too much marketing hype to believe it. Millennia of subtler, cultural communications prevent these important questions from being answered by the words in your proposal.

If you haven't taken the time and made the effort to build the trust, elevate your status, connect with the culture, emit the pheromones, overcome that peer pressure, generate the urgency and create the energy in the room, the words you've written aren't going to amount to much.

You can't bore clients into hiring you

A couple of questions for you:
Have you ever dozed off during a presentation?
Have you ever had anyone fall asleep in one of yours?

Since I'm guessing that you've had your own share of nodders and that you've at least dozed a little, I have to ask, "What's the point of putting together and practicing a presentation, then gathering all these people, if only to have them fall asleep?"

And since it's doubtful that the purpose of your presentation is to allow your audience to catch a few *zzzz*'s, I have to wonder why presentations are so incredibly boring?

It doesn't have to be this way! Audiences – and most especially your audience – should not have to endure such mind-numbing tedium – all of us reading bullet points together. No, if you're going to the trouble of planning, preparing and delivering a presentation, and if your audience is going to the trouble of assembling and sitting through it, it ought to be fabulous!

Way too many presenters try to cram way too much into their presentations. "Here are the 17 points I'd like to make today…" And it leaves us mind-numb, remembering nothing. Ask a member of any selection committee what they remember after all six short-listed firms have presented and they'll tell you that it all blended together into one long day of boredom.

David Ogilvy, the founder of Ogilvy & Mather Advertising once said, **"You can't bore people into buying your product."** Yet that might seem to be the objective when you watch the presentations that most firms deliver.

The secret to an engaging, memorable presentation is a simple, three-step method.

1. Make one point and make it well. The best presentations, the ones you remember for weeks, ask the audience to remember one and only one powerful point.
2. Bring your authentic self. Don't try to pretend to be somebody you're not. Don't pretend to be the gregarious game show host if, in fact, you're the quiet, analytical type. We want to meet and get to know YOU.
3. Bring enthusiasm. Don't tell us you're enthusiastic, or, as one firm did, have a bullet point slide that listed 'Enthusiasm!!!!' as one of their traits. We want to see your enthusiasm on show. If we can't see that you're excited about this project, we don't want you working on it.

Rather than boring your clients into submission, why not get them excited? Why not aim to have them talking about your presentation around the water cooler next day? Why not plan to put so much distance between your presentation and those limp attempts of all the other firms that they don't even try to catch up?

Stop phoning your presentations in. In this ballpark it's your 'A' game or go home.

Kylie Jenner, Real Madrid, Drake and LeBron James

Unless you've been living under a rock the names in that list are pretty familiar. In fact, all four are among the top 50 most followed on Instagram with poor LeBron trailing the pack with a paltry 30 million followers. Not coincidentally, they've all had some pretty impressive success on the business side of things, too.

The AE profession is a relative latecomer to the marketing game. It's laughable now, but it wasn't that long ago – well within the memory of many still active in the biz – that you could get your knuckles wrapped for publishing even the most modest ad. That kind of radical behavior was considered unethical.

Fortunately (or maybe unfortunately, depending on your point of view) those days are long behind us and we're now free to use the most creative, powerful and innovative marketing, business development and sales methods available. And the costs have plummeted too! You'd think we'd be dancing in the streets and taking full advantage of this kind of freedom.

Not here! Most firms are opting, instead, for traditional, dull, predictable, just-like-everybody-else marketing tactics. The kind that almost seem designed to confirm that our firm is not really any different than all the others. The core message of most marketing efforts can be summed up as, "Hire us, we do good work." Not very effective when everybody else does good work too. Imagine Drake building his brand by claiming, "Buy my music. I sing good songs."

As witnessed by the list at the top of this blog along with Under Armour, Apple, Disney and so many others, today's marketing is all about building a brand. For most AE firms, however, marketing is all about winning the next project. Which misses a most important point: Build a strong brand and the projects will walk in on their own. Because we've had our heads down, or perhaps assumed that it

210

doesn't apply to us, we've missed that important lesson.

To be sure, there are a small number of firms that are willing to play at the leading edge. Hats off to them for their daring. They deserve all the additional business they are winning!

Fortunately, we're surrounded by and exposed every day to a barrage of truly innovative marketing. Wanna see some? Turn on the TV. Open a magazine. Follow Dwayne (The Rock) Johnson on Instagram. Google, 'Best ad campaigns.' Mostly, stop looking at and copying other AE firms.

It's too easy to dismiss the incredible marketing that takes place in popular culture as being irrelevant to 'noble professionals.' But dismiss it at your own risk. The evidence that the traditional AE style of marketing has lost its effectiveness is clear in the fact that, despite a sizzling economy and a huge supply of work, fees aren't going up. Simple supply and demand should have them rising so something's amiss.

Drake knows how to sing, write, produce and act. So do thousands of other artists. But he also knows how to build and capitalize on a brand. We'd all do well to pay attention.

Trite and meaningless

D o you have any idea how boring it is to read proposals from AE firms? I mean, we're talkin' mind-numbing, skull-crushing, smack-me-in-the-head-to-see-if-I'm-still-alive monotony.

Every cover letter assures you that, **"We're pleased to have this opportunity to submit…"** Every firm claims to be **"uniquely qualified…"** Every team member will **"exceed your expectations…"**

I feel sorry for those clients who have to read all those lifeless, hackneyed and stodgy proposals. I really do. So a while ago I dreamed up what I call **'The Trite Test.'** Here's how it works:

If we assume that the bottom line of all marketing is differentiation, in other words, "What have you got that I can't get from everybody else?" it's reasonable that any statement you make should set you further apart from the pack. You can apply the Trite Test by asking this question:

"Could I imagine one of my competitors, in an effort to differentiate himself from me, writing the opposite of what I've just written?"

Let's try an example with a stale, worn-out statement that's used in virtually every proposal cover letter.

"Acme Engineers is pleased to submit this proposal…"

Apply the *Trite Test* and see if you can imagine someone writing the opposite:

"We're really ticked at having to prepare and submit this proposal."

Now, while it's sometimes closer to the truth, you'd never

actually write that. The fact that you were pleased to submit the proposal is self-evident. If you weren't pleased you wouldn't have bothered. So it's a cornball statement that adds nothing to your submission. And since every proposal from every one of your competitors starts with the same tired old sentence, clients predictably assume that you're all identical and decide to select on price.

How about another common example: **"We will exceed your expectations."** Apply the trite test and you get, **"You're likely going to be disappointed by our services."** Or the ubiquitous, **"We are uniquely qualified."** The trite test results in, **"We're pretty much the same as everybody else."**

Amusing when we look at it this way, but sad when clients see the same meaningless statements in proposal after proposal. They're tired of being subjected to that kind of colorless, repetitive twaddle.

And you should be tired of having your proposal look exactly like all the others.

How can you avoid these trite and meaningless statements? First, toss the old boilerplate. Most proposal efforts begin with 'Save As' and then edit a previous proposal (the boilerplate of which might date back a decade or more). Then set out to show this particular client how you're going to solve their problems and fulfill their desires on this particular project. Take the time to build a win strategy. Identify the client's hot buttons, then respond directly to them. Take the time to research the project's background and demonstrate the understanding and insight you're bringing to the table. Most of all, demonstrate the clear added value that the client, the stakeholders and the end users will enjoy when they choose to work with you.

Yes, it's more work. But your clients will thank you for showing them something different, something fresh, something that shows that there's a firm that has a pulse when it comes to writing proposals.

What's that smell?

Cognitive and communication researchers tell us that communication is enhanced when more of the senses are involved in receiving the message. In other words, you'll remember the conversation with your friend in more detail and for much longer if you're enjoying a warm latte while you chat.

A typical AE presentation engages only sight and hearing while the remaining three senses sit on the sidelines. But with each additional sense you involve you become more engaging and memorable.

I once coached a presentation that addressed environmental concerns regarding an endangered species of bats living in a cave on the project site. We brought jars of bat dung from the caves to the presentation and passed them around, inviting the audience to take a sniff. The combination of touch (feeling the weight and texture of the jar) and smell (this stuff is ripe!) locked our presentation into their minds in a way that mere sight and sound never could.

You can do the same thing. What can you bring to your next presentation that you can pass around for the audience to touch and hold? How about a soil sample? A piece of rusty old pipe that your project is going to replace? A circuit board from your control system? There are countless tangible 'artifacts' that you could bring to a presentation that not only engage additional senses, they help the audience understand what you do.

And they make your presentation more memorable.

When you bring that rusty old water pipe or concrete core, drop it on the table so they actually experience its weight and sound. When you pass the jar of raw materials around, invite them to touch or take a sniff (assuming it's not toxic of course!) and let them take away the memory of the power of what you do when you transform that material into a completed project.

214

Think about attending an outdoor concert. Think about sitting outside under the stars, smelling the blossoms, feeling the breeze, hearing the music. That sensory combination creates a memorable event that sticks in your mind forever. The more we can engage these senses, the more memorable your presentation becomes.

I've even brought warm chocolate chip cookies to a presentation. It was three o'clock in the afternoon, I knew that blood sugar would be low and everybody would be dragging a little. The cookies were a hit and the presentation more memorable as a result. I've even brought cold beer to a presentation to a real estate developer one hot Friday afternoon in July. (The beer was a hit too, but don't try this with your next presentation to the state DOT!)

Watching and listening to a presentation is the norm. But if you can augment those ears and eyeballs with touch, smell and taste, you're going to make an impression that lasts a long time.

14% of your clients are about to leave

A recent McGraw-Hill/AIA Large Firms Roundtable survey showed that 86% of design firm clients reported a high level of satisfaction with the quality of their projects and architects (and it's safe to extrapolate to engineers, too).

On the one hand, good job, folks!

On the other hand, that leaves 14% of clients out there who are a) unhappy with their providers, and b) open to looking for new firms to work with.

A firm that loses 14% of its clients each year is going in the wrong direction. Fast. But the firm that picks up the 14% who are looking for a better choice will have an impressive growth curve.

Over-the-top client service is the single biggest opportunity for you to differentiate your firm, keep the existing clients you have, attract new clients away from your competitors and grow in both volume and profits.

There are six key strategies that go into a world-class client service program. I'm pretty sure you're making the grade on one or two of them. But are you excelling at all six?

- Are you modeling the best service companies in the world? Not just your competitors in the AE industry, but the real global trend setters in all industries. What store is your personal favorite for customer service? What can you do to be more like them?
- Are you seeking regular and honest feedback? And when you get it, are you rationalizing, or taking them at their word and acting on the things they're less-than-pleased with?
- Are you making the most of those times when you drop the ball? We all screw up occasionally. The difference lies in what you do next.
- Do you have special pricing strategies for returning clients? Why shouldn't they get preferential treatment when they've shown you

their loyalty? The airlines, hotels and even little sandwich shops do it. What's holding you back?

- Are you giving your clients more than they ask for? "We'll exceed your expectations!" is about the most hackneyed, overused expression in the business. How often does it actually happen?

- Are you taking advantage of the incredible power of 'Thank You?' Your Mom taught you that 'please' and 'thank you' were magic words. She was right! But they're far too rare in the business world. Do you express appreciation often enough?

The 14% don't complain. They don't let you know they're dissatisfied. They don't whine or cry. They just leave.

If they're going to stay, that new 14% who show up for the first time need to see they're working with a firm that's substantially different than the one they just left.

We're really not listening to you

Whenever you get up to make a presentation, whether it's on the podium at a conference or in the interview for a project, there is always a temptation to cover all the bases. But if you want your presentation to have impact, to be remembered, to be persuasive, I encourage you to resist that temptation and decide that instead, you'll talk about just one thing.

I know you've got many points you want to make. And it's not often you get the microphone and everyone's attention. But the truth is, if you ramble we're going to tune you out. Having tuned you out we're going to instantly forget you and never give you another chance to share your ideas with us.

The most powerful speeches, the most memorable and engaging presentations are focused. They leave us with one compelling idea that rings in our minds long after the speaker sits down.

Most members of the audience fully expect to find you boring. They come into any presentation anticipating that the speaker will ramble, stumble and wander around. They expect to be checking their Instagram, texting their friends or otherwise drifting off.

Your job is to shock the heck out of them by being interesting and engaging. The secret to which is FOCUS.

Just last week I watched a presentation that promised to be incredibly dull. It was on using metadata and key words to improve search engine results. Trust me, I expected not only to be bored, but to actually be put to sleep! But the speaker surprised and delighted me by focusing on just one thing. I walked away having learned that long-tail keywords were the secret to getting to the front of the line.

I know that there is much more to SEO than that. But because the speaker focused so intently and with such authority on this one micro-topic, I left the session very impressed and fully prepared to hear what he no doubt has to say (with equal authority) about other aspects of this subject area. In other words, by focusing in one area, he captured and held my attention and established himself as an expert to be sought out.

Which, it seems to me, is kinda the goal.

Yes, you have many things to say. Yes, it might be a while before you are back at the podium. Yes, you are intelligent and thoughtful and love to demonstrate both qualities to us.

But try to tell us five things and we stop listening.

Focus! Focus! Focus!

Your clients pay a lot of money for you to plan their projects. They see paying you to think the whole thing through before they start pushing dirt and pouring concrete as a valuable investment

If it works for your clients, you, too, should understand the tremendous value in creating and following an intelligent plan for your marketing, business development and sales efforts. Far too many firms still use an approach that can best be described as, 'if it moves, we'll shoot at it.'

While no plan ever remains static from its first iteration, the planning process forces you to think about how you'll allocate the finite resources available for winning work and ensure the effort isn't wasted.

When preparing a marketing plan, your highest-value strategy is one that will narrow and focus your marketing efforts instead of spreading and diversifying them. While this may seem counter-intuitive – and it's certainly opposite to what many firms do – there is no question that focus always produces better results than diversification.

Imagine you're a military General on a battlefield with 5,000 troops at your disposal. Is it better to spread them out in a long line and yell, "Charge!" or to concentrate on one or two targets at a time? Obviously, if you dilute your resources too greatly, the impact you'll have on your targets becomes negligible.

The best strategy is to analyze your target markets, determine the 'sweet spots', those areas where you are most likely to have success. Focus the bulk of your resources there. Does this mean that you'll ignore opportunities from other market sectors? No. But you should treat those opportunistically rather than as strategic targets.

There's an old marketing rule of thumb that I like to call the 'Rule of Five.' It suggests that at any time you should have five key markets. Of these, three are strong and vital and responsible for the bulk of your revenues. One is a new and emerging market that you're beginning to invest in and expect to be a solid producer in two or three years. And the last is an older, mature market that no longer provides the same returns as it once did. Two or three years from now you won't likely be serving that marketing any more.

Is it always exactly five? Not always. But it sure as heck isn't just one. And it sure as heck isn't fifteen.

Encouraging the tall poppies

There are some fundamental truths that, in spite of their self-evidence, need to be repeated on a regular basis. One of those fundamental truths is that the core of marketing, the foundation on which all branding, business development and sales is built, is differentiation.

When your prospective client is looking to decide between you and anybody else, the question they want answered is, "What will I get from you that I won't get from them?" That's the bottom line of every single action you take when it comes to winning work.

So, what's it going to be for your firm?

- A longer, deeper relationship
- A higher level of trust
- A more enjoyable (less stressful) experience
- More specialized knowledge
- A greater reputation
- A friendly face
- More five-star reviews on Yelp
- A unique (and somehow better) process for getting it done
- Greater familiarity
- A lower price
- A measurably better outcome
- Prestige
- Reduced risk
- ???

Far too many firms rely on the 'we've-done-stuff-like-this-before-and-we-do-good-work' schtick. If there ever was a time when that was effective, it's long gone now. Every one of your competitors has done 'stuff like this' before. And every one of them does good

222

work, too.

The bar has been raised and you'll need to jump higher. This is true of every industry and profession in the world today. It used to be that carmakers promoted and sold automobiles on the basis of reliability. But imagine buying a new car today and having the salesperson reassure you that, "It'll start every morning!" Telling a prospective client that you'll get their project done on time and within budget amounts to the same, hackneyed reliability claim.

If you're at a loss to identify what it is that clients get from you that they don't from anybody else, why not ask a few of them? I've often heard firms report that they assumed a client chose them for one reason, but it turned out it was something else altogether. So ask, "Why did you select us?"

And then start promoting their answer to those prospects who haven't yet realized how great you really are.

Your slide deck is **NOT** your presentation

Some time ago I attended a program on the healthcare industry. It was held in a hotel ballroom with perhaps 200 people in the audience and some very smart, sophisticated speakers. A giant screen was at the front of the room and way off to the side, in a corner, in the dark, was a podium where each speaker stood to present.

One of the speakers was a medical doctor who was barely five feet tall. Of course she had no control over her height, but she stood in the dark with the podium almost up to her chin and a microphone in front of her face. Her presentation had dozens of PowerPoint slides filled with bullet points that she read out loud while we read silently.

I don't remember a word she said or even what she was talking about. Which is really too bad because she was a very intelligent person who probably had some important things to say. Yet none of it sunk in with the audience because we weren't able to connect with her as a person.

The goal of a presentation should be to provide information in a way that maximizes the audience's ability to process and engage with it. But cognitive psychologists tell us that one of the least effective ways to accomplish this is to have identical information arrive in both written and spoken form simultaneously. Which is exactly what PowerPoint (as it's most commonly used) does. There's a screen full of bullet points. As our ears are hearing the presenter read them aloud, our eyes are reading them silently. Net result? Nothing sticks.

Now let's add the physical dynamics of most presentations – the audience facing a screen with the presenter off to the side or with his or her back to them – and it's no wonder we rarely remember the content or frequently even fall asleep!

The best presentations are those in which the audience engages and connects with the presenter. In other words, whatever is on display in the way of slides, boards or props is NOT your presentation. YOU are the presentation.

Let's repeat that: whatever you have up on the wall is not the presentation. Your visuals simply reinforce, augment, decorate and supplement the message that you, personally, as a human being are bringing to the audience.

Taking it one step further, if the words on the wall will sufficiently convey your message, why are you bothering to make a presentation? Why not save everyone the hassle and just send a memo?

But you have important points to make and that fact that you're there, in the room, delivering them will drive those points home more forcefully, enthusiastically and persuasively. Your visual materials are there to enhance, support and reinforce the message that YOU, the real essence of the presentation, are there to express.

Heeeeere's Johnny!

As a team gets ready for an interview, I often hear them struggling to sort through the roles that various team members will take during the presentation.

"Bob's going to introduce us and talk about the history of the firm, then Tracy will spend five minutes going over our approach to this project. When she's done, Mike will review the case study on the Fairmont project and then hand off to Amanda who will wrap things up with a few slides showing some of our preliminary ideas for the site."

The net result of trying to find a role for everyone who needs to be at the interview can end up looking like a game of Whack-A-Mole, with heads popping up and down for the entire 45 minutes. Not comfortable. Not professional. Not impressive.

The best way to handle multiple presenters at an interview is to have a 'host' and a series of 'guests.'

Imagine it like *Jimmy Kimmel Live!* Jimmy is the host who 'owns' the show. He comes out first, does his monologue and then introduces and interviews a series of guests. Each guest brings his or her own unique information, knowledge and value and adds a richness and variety that makes the show interesting and entertaining.

In the same way, you should select a 'host'. Obvious choices are the Project Manager or a Principal. That person will take the lead throughout the interview, introducing the firm and delivering any opening comments. They can then go on to introduce and 'interview' the various 'guests,' who are the subject matter experts and might be from your firm or other subconsultants if they have something vital that needs to be addressed.

Just like on Jimmy Kimmel's show, the guests stick around after their segment so they can engage in the ongoing conversation. That way it's entirely natural for Tracy to jump back in with a few additional comments even after her section is finished.

Another benefit to this approach is that it dramatically reduces the stress of trying to remember your 'lines.' It's a whole lot easier to answer questions about your topic in an 'interview' situation than it is to stand up and deliver a speech.

When you get to the Q&A, the host invites the questions and can easily and comfortably direct the question to the 'guest' who's best equipped to answer it. Other 'guests' are also free to jump in with their comments if it's appropriate.

When the Q&A is done, the host can then close out the presentation with his or her final remarks, thank the guests for their contributions and thank the 'audience' for coming to the 'show.'

Whether you pretend you're Jimmy Kimmel, Samantha Bee or go way back to Johnny Carson, the 'host' and 'guest' model for your next presentation can eliminate the 'Whack-A-Mole' effect and let everyone feel more comfortable, all while tapping your best experts to talk about the topics that they're most suited to address.

How do you juggle chainsaws?

How do you juggle chainsaws?
With great talent, confidence and concentration
There are tremendous similarities between the chainsaw juggler and the Project Manager. Take your eye off the target, for even a moment, and things go horribly wrong. Do it successfully, though, and everyone is in awe.

Any Project Manager worth their Smartphone knows how to scope, schedule and budget projects, and steer them to successful completion. That's entry-level stuff. So what separates the good PMs from the truly great? What does it take to move beyond the 'kid's stuff' as a Seller-Doer?

If you've had the privilege of working with one of the real champions, you've seen them seamlessly integrate the 'doing' with the 'selling.' You've witnessed them bring in more than their share of new work all the while keeping clients happy, schedules controlled and budgets managed.

The best Seller-Doers have long since realized that success in project management equals success in business. And successful Project Managers do far more than merely drag their projects across the finish line. They get it that scope, schedule and budget compliance is merely the ante into the game.

They understand their responsibility for bringing in a steady supply of new projects. And they embrace that challenge. They aim higher and they've realized that a deeper set of skills and a broader outlook are required if they're to be successful and they excitedly seek to master those skills and outlooks.

Mostly, they see themselves as true Entrepreneurs.

An entrepreneur is a self-directed person who corrals and coordinates diverse talents and resources to service clients and return profits. This description will also fit most managers, but there's a key difference between an entrepreneur and a manager. While most

228

managers are capable and dedicated to their jobs, entrepreneurs always act as if they have a personal stake in it.

Entrepreneurs realize that, while they work together with a team to accomplish the goal, they, personally, are the driving force behind that team. While entrepreneurs may not, and often don't actually perform the work, they are personally responsible for the quality of the work, the satisfaction of the customer and the financial return to shareholders.

This attitude sets the performance bar high. Without an entrepreneurial attitude, it's easy to find countless reasons why the project will or did fail. The owner didn't supply the right information. The technical staff was incompetent. The permitting agency was too slow. The budget was inadequate.

An entrepreneur, on the other hand, knows that failure is not an option. If the project fails, the company fails and they stand to lose everything. In a similar way, entrepreneurial project managers know that if the job is to be done, it's up to them.

They accept no excuses and find ways to knock down the barriers to successful project completion.

Richard Branson, Oprah, Steve Jobs, Sara Blakely, the list goes on. Each one, self-made from scratch. These are my heroes. Who are yours?

Capturing the value of 'free'

I love getting free stuff. The feeling of walking away (legally!) with something that you haven't had to pay for is right up there with sunshine and blue skies.

There's free stuff everywhere you look: Coke is on sale at the grocery store: buy one, get one free. Stay one week at the Turtle Dove Resort, get a free couples massage. Buy a new car, get free oil changes for life.

It's interesting to note, however, that you rarely get something for free unless you've paid for something else. Try telling the grocery store that you only need one bottle of Coke, so you'll take the free one please. Hardly ever does anyone hand you something of value and say, 'It's yours!' without you first having paid for something else.

So let's decide that 'Free' simply means it isn't a line item on your bill. You paid for it, but it just didn't show up on the invoice.

There are two kinds of 'free.' The 'random act of kindness' sort of free only scores points if it's done anonymously. In our relentless efforts to make it to heaven, we've all been taught to do good deeds, but to do them quietly, without taking credit and you'll be rewarded later.

The 'good for marketing' kind of free, however, scores no points if no one knows about it. If you give your client something for nothing and they aren't aware of it, you don't get any goodwill credit.

What's all this got to do with your AE firm?

You give away stuff for free all the time. Project scopes that stretch into size XXL without corresponding fees, the advice you give away without compensation, the extra time you spend with your clients. All these represent your equivalent of 'buy one, get one free.' To make matters worse, your clients come to expect all the free stuff without having to pay.

Let's learn how to give away free stuff while enjoying the marketing benefits AND maintaining control.

When you write your next contract, include a clause that says something to the effect of, "This fee includes up to $2,000 of additional scope items that are not yet identified, at no additional charge." Then, when the client asks you for something that's outside the scope, remind them of their 'free' scope expansion and happily do the task. When the $2,000 (or whatever amount is appropriate) runs out, let them know they've had their free bottle of Coke and they'll have to pay for the next one.

Any time you do provide service without payment, memorialize it with an invoice. Create an invoice that documents the work done, the hours taken and the fee for services. Then take a red pen, cross out the bottom line, write "No Charge" in big red letters and mail it to the client. They'll be thrilled at the great customer service and the free stuff.

But they'll also catch on that you're monitoring the creeping scope. You'll get the goodwill points while building in a reluctance to let the scope expand into size XXL

Fake it till you make it

The ability to build and nurture a broad network of friends and business associates is the single, most common trait among successful people in any field.

But it doesn't come naturally to most of us. In my own career, I've had to work hard to overcome an inherent preference for fewer friends and the tendency to stay in my own quiet office instead of getting out there and mixing it up with the folks who can help me succeed.

But as my career developed I learned to watch and imitate the people who I could see were the gifted networkers. They were the ones who were comfortable with anyone, who made everyone they met feel instantly comfortable, welcome and important. It was obvious that I needed to watch these folks because they were the ones landing all the clients. And I learned early that power goes to those who bring in work!

The more I watched them, the more I realized that, for some, the skill of comfortable networking hadn't come naturally either. Turns out that many of those who appear to be naturally comfortable, gregarious networkers have had to learn, study and practice the art of business networking before they were able to master it.

And that's the key to success for the rest of us.

You've heard the term, "Fake it till you make it?" Well, it turns out that if we find a Master networker, observe them, question them and follow them around, we can start to imitate them. And the more we observe and imitate, the more comfortable we become with the same skills, same habits and same behaviors as they have.

Over the years I've observed these people carefully and worked hard to make a habit of doing what they do. And I've found that, when I imitate these masters of networking, I get the same business development results they do. I get the same, abundant supply of profitable work.

When we were kids we loved to play 'Pretend.' Whether it was Princesses, Pirates, Spacemen or Wonder Woman, we would dress up and, for that afternoon, we were convinced that we'd been transformed into someone else. When you 'pretend' to be a great networker for an hour, it might be uncomfortable. But if you do it again for an hour next week, and two hours the week after, it gets easier and you're more convinced about the charade. Pretend long enough and one day you'll realize that you aren't pretending anymore.

I've been watching these rare Masters for more than 25 years now. And, like all champions, they make it look easy. But I've found that, when I simply do what they do, it really is much easier than it first seemed.

Go/No Go economics

In the next three minutes (a little less if you're a fast reader) I'm going to lower your stress level, raise your proposal hit rate and save you thousands of dollars.

I've joked before about the fact that the easiest way to double your hit rate is to cut in half the number of proposals you submit. But there are some solid financial reasons for cutting back on the number of proposals you write. The first step in saving money and raising your hit rate is to stop chasing jobs that you're likely to lose.

I get it that the decision of whether to chase a project or not can be a tough one: If you don't chase it, you're guaranteed not to win it. But chasing everything that moves is an expensive, time-consuming and frustrating process. It's time to get wiser than that and there is a really solid economic argument for cutting way back on the number of proposals you write. Let's look at some hard numbers that ought to convince you to back off on your proposal activity.

Proposal costs vary widely depending on the size of the project, the degree of competition and the expectations of the client. But let's assume that your average cost to produce a competitive proposal is $7,500 – a number that's probably close to the middle of the pack in the industry for a competitive proposal.

Let's also assume that your hit rate is 35% (and that might be even a little higher than average in the AE industry). Based on these two numbers, every project that you win would have to produce a profit of $21,429 for you just to break even on the proposal costs of all the jobs you did not win.

Now let's assume that you've become quite disciplined and cut way down on the number of proposals you write. Additionally, you spend more time and more money on each one – let's push it to $10,000, which increases both the quality of your proposals and the likelihood of winning.

Using this strategy, your hit rate jumps up to 80%, which isn't at all unheard of by firms using these best practices. In this case, your breakeven point falls to just $12,500 – a little more than half of the previous number.

Let's recap: You cut back on the number of proposals you write, easing the pressure on your marketing staff and lowering your stress. Your marketing costs go down and you use the extra time and resources to raise the quality of your proposals. The result is that your hit rate and your profits both go up significantly. Not bad for just three minutes of reading!

The riskiest thing you can do

If you're serious about winning that next project you have two choices:

1. Play it safe, be predictable, and avoid offending anyone who might give your firm a black mark.
2. Grab their attention by the throat and throw them to the ground with your all-or-nothing approach that leaves them absolutely no choice but to select you.

Since every good coach knows the best defense is a good offense, I'm a big fan of the second strategy to win this particular game.

There is nothing easier in the AE industry than coming second. It must be easy because so many firms regularly accomplish it! You never hear, "we came fifth!" The point is, in this business, you either win or you lose. There is no such thing as second place, just one winner and a whole string of losers.

I believe that the riskiest thing you can do is to be normal, predictable and 'safe.' Why is that so risky? Because it's a guarantee that you'll look exactly like every other firm you're competing against. Which takes you to second place.

Right now, stop reading this and go grab some recent proposals you've submitted. While you're at it, pull up a couple of your presentations. I'll wait.

Now be honest — are they bold, or are they bland and ordinary? Do they demand attention? Or are you bored before you even crack the cover? What about your presentations? Would YOU want to sit through one?

There is no firm like yours. No one else has the unique talents, attitudes, creativity and fire-in-the-belly that you have. So why don't those selection committees get it? They don't get it because we

236

chicken out and default to the familiar, boring stuff that we've always done.

I have a client who (once) tried something really different in a presentation. It was radical, remarkable, even outrageous. But they also felt they had nothing to lose, so they went for it. The client loved it and awarded them the project.

Since that time, though, they've had no end of excuses as to why that was a one-off situation, why that radical approach won't work for any other client, why they shouldn't try it with a client they don't know.

I've no doubt that, at some point, you've had a really whacko idea for a presentation. Or there was something truly outrageous that you wanted to include in your proposal. But you chickened out because you felt that the client wouldn't know how to take it. Or they might find it too far outside the norm. Regardless, you left that fantastic idea on the cutting room floor and went with the old predictable stuff.

Once, just once, I dare you to try that wild and crazy idea. I challenge you to stand up and let that client know exactly how amazing you are. I'm talking jaw-on-floor, hand-it-to-you-on-the-spot tactics that your competition would never have the nerve to try!

If second place is good enough for you, don't bother. But if your goal is winning, then the riskiest thing is to be predictable, to play it safe. It's a guarantee of coming second.

Focus on the benefits

When Steve Jobs introduced the first iPod, he didn't say, 'here we have an MP3 player with 5gb of memory, running on a PP5002 chip...

He said, '1,000 songs in your pocket.'

Now let's look at this same concept, but outside the world of technology. I went shopping for a new suit not long ago. A reasonably mundane experience, but one that emphasized a point that top presenters and marketing professionals have understood since the first caveman sold his friend a club.

As I examined suits in the first store, the salesman was eager to give me all the reasons I should buy my suit from him.

"Our suits are made from only the finest wool."

"Our tailors are all trained in Europe!"

"Our suits come with a one year satisfaction guarantee."

When I looked at suits in the second store, there was a subtle, but very important difference in the way the salesman spoke.

"The top-quality wool in this suit means you won't have to worry about wrinkles when you're traveling."

"The cut of the jacket, which our tailors learned in Europe, really compliments your features."

"If you're not satisfied, you can simply return the suit any time in the next year."

Where the first salesman focused on the product I was about to buy and related all the features of the suit, the second salesman went an important step further.

He turned the features of the suit into direct benefits to me.

He understood that I didn't care so much what the suit was made of as I did what it would look like when hauled out of a suitcase after a cross-country flight. He knew that the tailors could have come from Mars as long as the suit made me look good. And he knew I wanted the convenience of returning the suit if I discovered it did not meet my expectations.

Steve Jobs understood that technology appeals to technical people. The rest of us just want the benefit. When giving a technical presentation it's vitally important to be clear about the benefits to your audience. 'So What?' they'll want to ask, and you need to answer that question clearly.

Empty buildings and muddy trenches

A picture is worth 1,000 words. But those words will say nasty things about your firm if you don't choose and use your images wisely.

I can't count the number of times I've seen photos included in proposals, presentations, on websites and even in printed brochures that are just plain awful. Heavily pixilated, out of focus and boring are the most common offenses. But there are other transgressions that border on the criminally dumb too.

Low resolution photos – even the least expensive cell phone today can capture a digital image that is capable of being blown up to billboard proportions. So why do I see so many photos that look more like an ancient Greek mosaic? If the digital image isn't large enough to blow up without pixilation, don't use it. Take it again at a higher resolution or find another.

Poorly composed photos – there are a few simple rules of visual composition that anyone can learn in about three minutes. Have good visual balance, don't cut off important elements of your image, find an angle that lets the light enhance the subject in the best way. Google 'how to take a good photo' and share the information around the office.

Boring photos – there is nothing the least bit engaging about a photo of a piece of PVC pipe lying in the bottom of a muddy trench. But that's what I encounter when I look at the project experience sheets from countless civil engineering firms. The other disciplines have their own versions of these predictable pics. Yes, it might be a photo of the project, but there's a reason we end up burying this stuff – it's not nice to look at! We put the pipe there for the benefit it brings: Clean water from a tap. So let's have a photo of a cute three-year old enjoying a glass of cold water on a hot summer day.

Photos without people – the architects are the worst offenders on this one. It always seems that we wait until 5 AM on a Sunday to take the photo to make sure there isn't a living, breathing sentient being within five miles of the project! I know there are rules about signing waivers for people in photos, but get the staff from your office or hire your cousin to sit on the bench. The project was designed to accommodate humans – let's see a few populating it!

Photos without captions – flip through any magazine and you'll see that every photo has a caption. That's because we are too busy (or lazy) to read the articles. So we look at the pictures and read the captions. The client reviewing your proposal is no different. And don't have the caption simply say, "New 14-inch watermain along Main Street." Instead, let them tell a story: "Smith and Jones worked hard to keep the business owners along Main Street informed and up-to-date as the new watermain project progressed."

If you don't have compelling and engaging photos of the project, use some high quality, life-style photos that show people living the great life that your infrastructure project helps support. Or mix and match some life-style photos in with your more technical shots. There are many great stock photography websites that have high quality, royalty-free images at really low prices.

Poor quality photos in your marketing and business development efforts look unprofessional, amateurish and cheesy – not traits that make clients want to rush to hire your firm.

Four-letter words

Let's face it, we all have to sell

Or maybe we should avoid that four-letter word and say that we all have to persuade others to buy our services.

Whatever term we use, I regularly run into many business developers and seller-doers who are shy about selling. "I don't want to appear pushy." "I don't like coming across as a 'hard seller."

I want you to stop apologizing for selling your services to clients. I understand those sentiments and I, too, will never push something on someone who really doesn't want it. But I invite you to adopt a different point of view. One that just might revolutionize your attitude towards business development. Here's how it works…

Think back to a project you did a couple of years ago. Make sure you pick one that was really successful, the client loved it and everybody walked away a winner. And make sure it was at least two years back. Got it?

OK, now think about the fee you were paid.

Have you spent it? Do you still have any of that money hanging around? Are you still deriving benefit from the fee that client paid? Or, do you have to find other projects in order to keep the cash flowing? My guess is that the money's long gone. It was nice while it lasted, but let's face it, that was two years ago…

Finally, I want you to think about your client. Are they still enjoying the results of the work you did? Is the project still providing returns, benefits and positive cash flow? I'm sure they've long since stopped thinking about the fee they paid (regardless of the griping they did at the time!) but they're surely still glowing about how smart they were to do the project and to hire you to do it!

So who's the biggest winner?

The fact is that your clients ALWAYS come out ahead when they hire you. And that reluctance you have about selling? Kinda misdirected, isn't it?!

So, is the sales process something you do **to** somebody? Or something you do **for** somebody?

Don't talk to strangers!

Power goes to those who bring in work. So goes an old adage in the AE business. And it's a good one. Without a steady supply of profitable work, your firm won't be around much longer. And a big part of bringing in a steady supply of profitable work is regular and persistent networking and general client 'schmoozing.' But how do we overcome that pervasive reluctance, reticence and general bashfulness that afflicts far too many design professionals?

According to psychologists, fully half of the population self-identifies as being shy. But interestingly, only about 15% to 20% are visibly shy to a casual observer. That means that all those people you see who appear to be so much more confident than you are just as, if not more, nervous than you as you stand in the doorway of that networking event.

Even if they don't label themselves as shy, just about everyone has some level of fear when it comes to networking. What will I say? What if they ignore me? What should I talk about? These kinds of nervous questions aren't just in your mind. They're in everyone else's too.

The bad news is that reticence can keep you from making the connections and building the relationships that will help advance your career and your company. The good news is that most shyness is learned behavior, which means that it can be un-learned and replaced with more productive and useful habits. How can you change those habits?

Some of our introversion is natural, but some has been taught – by your Mom, of all people! She (quite correctly) taught you not to speak to strangers. Which is really good advice when you're walking home from school at seven years of age. But it's terrible advice when you're 37 and working a trade show, mingling at a conference reception or trying to make some business development progress.

244

To overcome this old instinct, we need to redefine the term 'Stranger.' When you're attending a meeting of professional colleagues you're not really with strangers at all. At any gathering, you have many common interests with the others there. Although you may not have met them before, you have a lot in common: the engineering profession, improving municipal infrastructure, the association that's hosting the reception, the traffic on the way to the meeting…

So before you arrive at the event or the meeting, spend some time thinking about what you have in common. Identifying the common ground makes you feel more comfortable and can help you break the ice. These common interests can launch a conversation with someone who might become your new best client.

A 'stranger' used to be anyone you'd never met. But if you hang on to that definition and the admonition your Mom gave you, you won't make much progress as a business developer. By redefining the term 'stranger,' you can open the door to many new and potentially beneficial relationships.

Qualifications-based selection is dead

The Brooks Act was passed in 1972. This landmark and oh-so-needed legislation required that the U.S. Federal Government (and subsequently many state and local governments) select engineering and architecture firms based upon their competency, qualifications and experience rather than by price.

Well done, Congressman Brooks!

But times have changed. In the intervening 45 years the AE profession has become much more sophisticated, proficient and amazingly capable. Whereas in 1972, there may only have been a few firms competent and qualified to properly execute a particular project, today there are dozens, if not hundreds of fully qualified firms lining up to propose on every project. The truly incompetent are eliminated quickly and those who remain are, as often as not, every bit as capable as every other firm in contention.

In this situation you have a long line of competitors, each of whom is fully capable of doing the project and doing it well. If you don't want to go the low-fee route, what are your options?

Traditional AE marketing, the kind that's been in use since the days of the Brooks Act, promotes the firm based on its technical merits. The other day I saw an ad that a firm had placed in an industry journal that summed it up perfectly – "Our work stands for itself." This is a wonderful sentiment and there's no doubt that that firm is highly capable. But so are its competitors.

In a world in which all firms that are in reasonable contention for a project are essentially equal, we've created the economic definition of a commodity. We've come full circle back to 1972 and clients have no choice but to select on price.

So, how do you overcome the traffic jam at the top of the 'qualified' list? What do you do when qualifications alone are no longer enough?

The surprisingly simple answer comes from some unexpected

experts who have overcome the same challenge. Think about the Kardashians, a group of perfectly ordinary people who set out to build a brand. Think about Geico Insurance and the marketing dominance it's achieved by simply making more noise than its competitors.

All this might make you uncomfortable, if not irate. Isn't there a world of difference between professional design services and discount car insurance? Perhaps. But to compete and prevail in a world where the differences in technical qualifications and experience between firms are negligible you need to adopt a different marketing strategy that will help you stand out in a very crowded market. And I'm not above learning valuable lessons no matter where I find them.

Congressman Brooks did the industry a huge favor. But 45 years is a long time and 1972's solution doesn't work so well now. Competing and marketing based on your technical merits alone, letting your work stand for itself, are no longer enough.

As hard as it is to swallow, today's marketing has to appeal as much to emotion as it does to intellect.

Planning to win

We're smack in the middle of football season. Every week it's a new match-up and the fans are all hoping for the win. The coaches and players, on the other hand, are **planning** for the win.

Imagine this scenario: It's game day and the coach walks into the locker room to tell the team, "Just run the same plays that we ran last week. It worked for us then, I'm sure it'll work for us now."

That would be ludicrous! No coach would ever head into a game without first studying the opposition, reviewing his team for who's at the top of his game and who's on the disabled list, then coming up with a game plan to create advantage, to build a strong offense, an ironclad defense and the best chance of winning.

As ludicrous as it would be for a coach to simply recycle old game plans, that's exactly what most AE firms do as they head into a proposal. Their win strategy consists of hitting, 'Save As' while they recycle an old proposal. It's no wonder that the average hit rate is below 30 percent! The old-fashioned, 'Save As' method fails because it doesn't recognize that each client, each project, each opportunity is different.

The game plan that the coach prepares is unique to next Sunday's game and only to next Sunday's game because the conditions, the opposition and the alignment of the planets are only that way once. There isn't one plan that's suitable for every game and there isn't one proposal that's suitable for every RFP. If you're not developing a unique win strategy for each proposal, it's a guarantee your success rate will never be as high as you want it to be.

If you head into a proposal effort without first putting together a detailed win strategy, you're playing blind. You might just as well throw in the towel at the start of the first quarter.

The AE world has changed dramatically. Client loyalty has dried up. Competition is intense. And you're being treated like a commodity. This, in spite of the economy singing along like gangbusters. You need every advantage you can get and developing a win strategy for every proposal gives you a whole heap of advantage.

No one can guarantee a win. Not the Patriots, not the Astros or Dodgers and not you. But as Bill Belichick would tell you, the team that creates the best game plan usually wins.

Letting your warts show

We all know them. They're the sorts who, after they've dropped the ball, go to great lengths to assure us it wasn't their fault and deflect the blame to some other poor schmuck. The saddest thing about this kind of person is the utter transparency of their efforts. Usually, the fault is so obvious that their efforts to duck responsibility would be humorous if they weren't so despicable.

The one thing we all have in common with this poor sap is that we screw up. Regularly. And sometimes in a really big way. What separates us is what we do after we step in the doo-doo.

Who would you rather work with: The person who makes a mistake, then tells you why it wasn't really a mistake, why it doesn't matter and why it actually wasn't their fault? Or the person who comes to you, tells you they've made a mistake (often before you find out on your own) and tells you what they're going to do to fix it? Your clients would rather work with that person too.

When you try to hide a problem you've created or deflect the blame elsewhere, the trust that others have in you disappears. But when you step up and face the music, your credibility takes a huge leap. "If she's being honest with me about this, I've got to believe she's going to be honest with me about everything." It doesn't feel very good in the moment, but the long-term benefits are enormous.

Sure it's embarrassing to screw up. We all want to appear to be perfect and our egos take a big hit when we fall short of the mark. Our first instinct is to hide and hope no one notices. But then, when someone does notice, our second instinct is to make excuses or point the finger elsewhere. Every one of these actions simply digs the hole deeper, making it that much harder to climb out in the end. As much as it goes against your survival instincts, resist the temptation to duck, cover up or deflect. It makes you look like the two-year old who covers his eyes and thinks that nobody can see him.

Your client knows you're not infallible. They know you're going to make mistakes.

When you make that inevitable mistake, that's the time to show what you're really made of. Step up right away, tell the truth about what happened, then tell what you're going to do about it. It isn't that you screwed up. It's about what you do after it hits the fan.

When you mess up, 'fess up. This is a golden opportunity to set yourself truly apart from everyone else.

Times change. Deal with it.

In some ways it's like watching your grandfather contemplate the latest iPhone. He kind of shakes his head, mutters something about back-in-the-day and gets a wistful look in his eye as he realizes that his time has come and gone.

Here's the version of that story I hear almost daily, accompanied by the same melancholy look:

"We had projects walking in the door for decades with almost no marketing effort."

"Our reputation was all we ever needed."

"Our founder and CEO brings in all the work. Everybody loves him! He's retiring next year."

"Our clients are treating our services as a commodity."

"None of our technical professionals like to sell."

Nostalgia and sentimentality are nice around the holidays, but they won't bring profitable work in your door. Sure, it was fun while it lasted. This is the new normal of today and any firm that does not step up to the challenge of these new realities will go the way of your grandfather's hand-cranked phone.

Marketing – non-stop, over-the-top, aggressive and intelligent marketing – is an absolute necessity. And that doesn't mean simply cranking up the number of RFPs you respond to. That gets you nothing but a lower hit rate. It means embracing a marketing and sales culture, engaging marketing professionals and learning as much about marketing as you know about engineering or architecture.

As you begin to think ahead to 2018, here are four non-negotiable must-do's if you want to be telling a different story in 12 months.

1. Differentiate! Find something – anything! – that sets your firm apart from the crowd. Clients treat you as a commodity

because all the firms you compete with look and sound and act EXACTLY the same. I don't care if you become known as the firm that drives around in pink trucks, so long as you do something to set yourself apart.

2. Build your brand! Within the design professions, branding is the least understood, least utilized and yet most powerful marketing tool available. The day in which you can say that it only works for beer and soap and cars is over. Yes, it works wonderfully for them. And the same principles can work for you too. Learn about the power of branding. Then leverage it to your advantage.

3. Write fewer proposals! But make them intelligent, clever and laser-targeted. It's long since been proven that throwing lots of proposals out there is a really bad way to win work. It costs a lot of money, it frustrates your marketing coordinators no end, and it simply doesn't work.

4. Get serious about business development! And get comfortable with an unpopular four-letter word: SELL! Yes, design professionals have to sell, sell regularly and sell hard. Selling requires a set of skills that wasn't taught in engineering or architecture school and you need to learn, practice and hone those skills daily. The founding CEO can't and won't do it forever.

Your grandfather will manage just fine without an iPhone. But you have no choice when it comes to embracing a marketing and sales culture if you want to survive and thrive in this game.

How fast do you fail?

A 12-month-old baby knows a lot about failure. Every time she lets go of the coffee table to attempt a step or two – thump! Failed again. Of course the easiest way for our cute little one to avoid failure is to give up on the idea of walking. It would be so much easier to just sit and let Mom bring the bottle.

There are a couple of reasons why that toddler keeps trying. First, the world looks pretty big and exciting and you can cover a lot more ground on two feet than on all fours, so it's worth the effort. But more importantly, she hasn't yet got the memo that failure is a bad thing. There's no shame in falling on your butt when you're 12 months old. In fact we grown-ups think it's pretty darn cute.

But by the time we've grown up, been formally educated, got a job and taken responsibility for an engineering firm, they've managed to thoroughly convince us that failure is the worst possible option, to be avoided at all costs. And that's when most growth and learning stops.

Most design firms that I see spend an inordinate effort to avoid failure of any kind. Which, don't get me wrong, is a pretty good idea when you're designing a bridge or a building. But it's a major obstacle when you're trying to grow a company. By assiduously avoiding failure, we also avoid innovation, creativity, growth and breakthrough thinking. We stay carefully in the rut we occupy and discourage looking from side to side.

The best companies on the other hand, the ones we all wish we could be like, encourage, embrace and endure failure on their way to success. And the faster they fail, the quicker they grow.

Painfully few firms seek regular feedback from their clients. Even fewer invite their clients and end users into the decision making process as they evolve their companies. Of the thousands of firms I've encountered I would estimate that fewer than 10 percent even have an outside member on their Board of Directors.

Wanna fail faster?

- Set up a Board of Advisors entirely made up of people from outside your firm.
- Establish a Brain Trust, whose job it is to push you into places you might not be brave enough to go on your own.
- Host quarterly client feedback forums in which they feel free to tell you what they really think and share the great ideas that are apparent from the other side of the table.
- Fail regularly, then get up, brush yourselves off and carry on, having learned invaluable lessons.

That toddler knows far more about failure than you or I do and she's not afraid of it. That's why she learns faster, grows quicker and laughs more often. When was the last time you were glad you failed?

Last Thoughts

When it comes right down to it, marketing is actually pretty simple. In fact, you could sum it all up in just three steps.

1. What makes you special?
   What do you offer to your clients that they simply can't get anywhere else? What do they find in you, your firm, the services you offer, the knowledge you have, the process you use, the attitude you bring, that they can't find on every street corner? If you can define that special something, you're already more than halfway to success.

   But...

   Don't rest on your laurels. Because as soon you find success with that unique specialness, somebody's going to copy you at a lower price and you'll have to find that NEXT special something.

2. What's in it for me?
   Clients don't care how long you've been in business, that your founder was born in a log cabin, that you have 26 offices in 14 states or that you've updated your logo. They only care about how their life is going to be better when they work with you. So, tell them.
   Tell them how their risk will be reduced, their bottom line enhanced, their status increased, their employees happier, their children safer, their patients healthier and their constituents more likely to vote for them. They don't want to buy what you sell. They want to buy their own happiness and security.

3. Over, and over, and over again.
   There are a lot of competitors out there. And they're all
   clamoring for your client's attention. The minute you stop
   building your brand, promoting your firm, connecting with
   your target market, is the minute they begin to forget about
   you and start thinking that the next firm is the next big thing.
   Keep an eye on Toyota, Google, McDonald's and Amazon.
   Even massively successful, long-established companies like
   these realize that promotion and brand-building never stop.

   Your presence in the marketplace is like the hole that's
   formed when you stick your hand into the bucket of water.
   Pull it out and see how long the hole lasts.

Yeah, it's work, but it can also be a whole lot of fun. Make sure
you're having plenty along the way.

About David A. Stone

One of the leading marketing thinkers in the AE industry, David Stone has advised hundreds of design and construction firms around the globe ranging in size from one person to $2 billion in annual revenue. He is the author of 15 books including *[re]wired*, which is used in the CPSM certification program. He is a sought-after speaker at design and construction conferences around the world. With a career that began in architecture in the mid-70s, David has held every position from Draftsman to Principal. He has witnessed and dealt with the massive changes this industry faces and continues to explore new ways to promote and sell design and construction services.